Travel Guide

PARIS

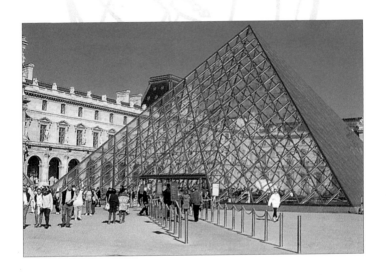

MELISSA SHALES

NEW
HOLLAND

NEW
HOLLAND

```
★★★ Highly recommended
 ★★ Recommended
  ★ See if you can
```

Fourth edition published in 2005
by New Holland Publishers (UK) Ltd
London • Cape Town • Sydney • Auckland
First published in 1996
10 9 8 7 6 5 4 3 2

website: www.newhollandpublishers.com

Garfield House, 86 Edgware Road
London W2 2EA, United Kingdom

80 McKenzie Street
Cape Town 8001, South Africa

14 Aquatic Drive, Frenchs Forest,
NSW 2086, Australia

218 Lake Road, Northcote,
Auckland, New Zealand

Distributed in the USA by
The Globe Pequot Press
Connecticut

Keep us Current
Information in travel guides is apt to change, which
is why we regularly update our guides. We'd be
grateful to receive feedback if you've noted something we should include in our updates. If you have
new information, please share it with us by writing
to the Publishing Manager, Globetrotter, at the office
nearest to you (addresses on this page). The most
significant contribution to each new edition will
receive a free copy of the updated guide.

Publishing Manager (UK): Simon Pooley
Publishing Manager (SA): Thea Grobbelaar
DTP Cartographic Manager: Genené Hart
Editors: Melany McCallum, Thea Grobbelaar,
Geraldine Christy
Cartographers: Genené Hart, Nicole Bannister
Design and DTP: Nicole Bannister, Philip Mann,
ACE Ltd
Consultant: Steve Fallon
Reproduction by Hirt & Carter (Pty) Ltd, Cape Town
Printed and bound by Times Offset (M) Sdn. Bhd.,
Malaysia.

Although every effort has been made to ensure that
this guide is up to date and current at time of going
to print, the Publisher accepts no responsibility or lia-
bility for any loss, injury or inconvenience incurred
by readers or travellers using this guide.

Acknowlegdements:
The author would like to thank the following people
for their generous assistance in the preparation of this
book: Penelope Shales, who helped enormously with
expert knowledge of Paris and all things French, lent
me numerous books and shot many of the photos for
the book; Dennis Hudson and Dominic Shales, who
also helped with pictures; Kirker European Travel,
British Midland, the Hôtel St Augustin and
Disneyland Paris who all helped with facilities.

Photographic credits:
Peter Adams/jonarnold.com, cover; **David Alexander**,
page 24; **Jon Arnold/jonarnold.com**, page 66; **Jacqui
Cordingley**, pages 23, 56 (top); **Peter Feeny**, pages 6,
18, 95; **Brian Harding**, pages 10, 107, 112; **Glenn
Harper**, pages 22, 96; **Roger Howard**, pages 59, 62,
105; **Hudson/ Shales**, pages 7, 8, 40, 42, 44, 45, 46, 48,
49, 52, 56 (bottom), 57, 58, 71, 88 (top), 99; **Caroline
Jones**, page 4; **Gordon Lethbridge**, page 79; **David
Lund**, pages 63, 82; **Peter Baker/PhotoBank**, page 25;
Norman Rout, pages 11, 35, 109, 111; **Neil Setchfield**,
pages 19, 38; **Melissa Shales**, pages 12, 15, 16, 17, 20,
21, 30, 32, 34 (top and bottom), 37, 43, 51, 65, 72, 74,
75, 80, 81, 83, 84, 87, 88 (bottom), 89, 90, 91, 93, 98, 102;
Stuart Spicer, pages 9, 33, 68; **Jeroen Snijders**, pages
26, 28, 29, 100 (top and bottom), 101; **Chris Warren**,
title page, pages 27, 55, 60, 67, 73, 76.

Cover: *Notre Dame, an architectural masterpiece .*
Title Page: *Glass pyramid, entrance to the Louvre.*

CONTENTS

1
Introducing
Paris

A city of crowned heads and severed heads, with soaring architectural triumphs, from the glorious Cathedral of Notre Dame to the magnificence of Versailles and the avant garde spectacle of the Georges Pompidou Centre, Paris is superb. Dramas, melodramas, great tragedies and comedies have all been enacted here, on and off the stage. The city has decided the fate of kings and empires and has nurtured many of the world's greatest artists, writers, philosophers and musicians. Every age has left a legacy of splendid monuments and gracious churches. Rulers of France, from Charles V to Napoleon III and President Mitterrand, have understood that their place in posterity is measured in stone, and Paris, more than any other European city, has a centuries-old, ongoing love affair with beautiful and innovative architecture. Yet the real magic of Paris comes not only from these magnificent creations, but from the shuttered, balconied boulevards, the winding backstreets, the small squares and the avenues of square-cut trees.

It is a city to be savoured slowly. Take comfortable shoes, decide on an area, then wander. Allow yourself time to enjoy the flower seller beside a tiny wrought-iron fountain, the brightly canopied pavement café rich with the smell of aniseed and fresh coffee, a subtly carved stone doorway, the statuesque mime artist perched on a concrete bollard. It is almost impossible to get lost. If your feet collapse under you, you will never be far from a metro. And if you haven't seen all the top ten sights, it doesn't really matter. They will still be there next time.

TOP ATTRACTIONS

*** Arc de Triomphe: Napoleon's monument to his own power.
*** Eiffel Tower: the world's most famous radio transmitter.
*** The Louvre: palace and gallery extraordinaire.
*** Cathedral of Notre Dame: a glory of the Gothic era.
*** The Sainte-Chapelle: St Louis' dazzling glass chapel.
*** Musée d'Orsay: one of the world's finest art collections.
*** Montmartre: artists, cafés and the can-can.

Opposite: *The Eiffel Tower seen from the Palais de Chaillot.*

Above: *Notre Dame dominates the Île de la Cité in the midst of the Seine. The foundation stone of the cathedral was laid in 1163 by Pope Alexander III.*

THE LAND

It is the works of man, not nature, that have given Paris its unique charm, yet the surrounding landscape, a low-lying plain in northern France, is gentle and fruitful with a light that has inspired generations of artists. The ancient Celts chose to build here for logistic and practical reasons. The river gave them excellent transport and a good supply of water and fish. The area is a natural trading crossroads and the islands were easily defended in a landscape virtually devoid of hilltops. It is still well situated for travel and transport throughout Europe.

Central Paris, defined by its terrifying ring road, the Boulevard Périphérique, covers a comparatively small area of about 105km^2 (40 sq miles) and has a population of around 2,250,000. It lies at the heart of the roughly circular Île de France, which, in spite of its name, is not an island but defines the tiny area that was the personal domain of the early kings.

Today, the Île de France, covering about 14,500km^2 (5600 sq miles), is made up of eight *départements*: Paris, Seine-et-Marne, Yvelines, Essonne, Hauts-de-Seine, Seine-St-Denis, Val-de-Marne and Val-d'Oise. Much of it is now effectively 'Greater Paris', covered by commuter towns and high-rise suburbs. With over 11 million inhabitants (almost a fifth of the country's population), it is the most densely populated region of France.

The Seine

Defining the geography, architecture and whole fibre of Paris, the River Seine loops slowly through the heart of the city for 12km (7^1/$_2$ miles), languidly accepting all tributes, including its elevation to World Heritage Site status. The river rises on the Langres Plateau, northwest of Dijon, and meanders gently across the country, moving slowly as it drops only 470m (1543ft) during its 775km (480 mile) journey from source to sea, at Le Havre on the Channel coast.

Paris, many miles inland, is still the fourth largest port in France (after Marseilles, Le Havre and Dunkirk) and the river is alive with traffic. The working docks are away from the centre in Gennevilliers and Charenton, but heavily laden barge trains groan slowly through the city, whole families living aboard; colonies of houseboats thrive along the banks; and a seemingly endless parade of sightseeing boats ply the river by day and night (*see* page 120), adding to the gaiety.

For nearly 2km (1^1/$_4$ miles) the river is bordered on both sides by double-decker quays, the earliest of which, the quai des Grands Augustins, was built by Philip IV (the Fair) in 1313. Lined above by knobbly plane trees and below by cool, green poplars, the quays are wonderful for walking and picnics, although part of the right bank has now been usurped by a busy motorway. Through the city centre are also 36 bridges, the oldest, ironically called the Pont Neuf (New Bridge), opened in 1607 (*see* page 35). The most flamboyant , the Pont Alexandre III, with pillars surmounted by gilded statues, was built for the 1900 World Exhibition (*see* page 72).

THE ZOUAVE

The first Pont de l'Alma was built in 1856, to celebrate Napoleon III's victory in Crimea, but eroded so badly that a shiny new steel version was erected in 1972. Only one column of the old bridge remains, adorned by a statue of a Polish Second Empire soldier, now known as the Zouave. He has become the city's official bench mark, used to measure the height of the Seine in times of flood. The highest on record is when the water reached his chin in January 1910. He is best seen from a boat.

Below: *The Zouave on the Pont de l'Alma is on permanent sentry duty in case of flooding.*

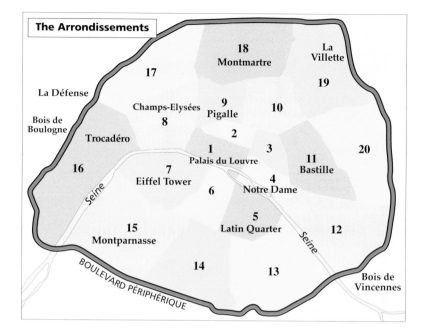

The Arrondissements

18 Montmartre

La Villette

17

19

La Défense

Champs-Elysées
8

9
Pigalle

10

Bois de Boulogne

Trocadéro

2

16

1
Palais du Louvre

3

11
Bastille

20

7
Eiffel Tower

4
Notre Dame

6

Seine

Seine

15
Montparnasse

5
Latin Quarter

12

BOULEVARD PÉRIPHÉRIQUE

14

13

Bois de Vincennes

Below: *Traditional flower stalls are still a romantic option in this bustling modern city.*

The Arrondissements

Nineteenth-century Paris was a lawless place, seething with rebellion, no matter who was in power. There was little chance of keeping control in the narrow, winding streets, so easily blockaded and so very difficult for moving troops. Napoleon III, aware of his tenuous grasp on power, determined to try to impose discipline on the unruly mob and on the very layout of the city. Between 1852 and 1870 his Prefect of the Seine, Baron Georges Haussmann, began to remodel Paris, literally sweeping away large sections of the city, sending over 200,000 poor people to live out of sight in a ring of shanty suburbs. On the Île de la Cité alone 25,000 people were moved and throughout Paris thousands of homes and many outstanding buildings were demolished. The main streets were broadened and straightened, parks created, a proper underground sewer system constructed, and the opera house and railway stations built. From Haussmann's

vision rose modern Paris, an elegant, bourgeois city of wide, tree-lined boulevards and open spaces, offering an uncluttered view of many of the major monuments.

Among the many structures to tumble were the city walls, their space used to create a ring road, the Boulevard Périphérique. For the first time the whole area within this circle was incorporated into the Ville de Paris and the districts were redivided into 20 arrondissements. The system is still in use today, starting at the heart of Paris, the Louvre, with the first arrondissement, and spiralling out clockwise to the twentieth. Anything outside the Périphérique is counted as a suburb. This system makes it easy to learn your way around the city. All street signs and maps mark the arrondissement alongside the name.

THE SUBURBS

The suburbs have an odd mixture of styles and all seem rather unplanned, with 50-year-old villas next to soulless apartment blocks. La Défense is ultra-modern, Neuilly is elegant, St-Denis surrounds a great medieval basilica, while American-style houses squat oddly round the palace in Versailles. On the whole, the more elegant suburbs are to the west, the poorer areas to the east, although the advent of Disneyland Paris with its facilities and excellent transport has shifted the balance to some extent.

Above: *Street sign displaying the number of the arrondissement. Many streets are named after celebrated French men and women.*

Arrondissement by Arrondissement

First Rich and royal Paris, with the Louvre, part of the Île de la Cité, and serious shopping at the Forum des Halles and the Rue St Honoré.

Second The financial centre, surrounding the Bourse (Stock Exchange) and the old Bibliothèque Nationale (National Library).

Third Delightfully villagey, with the narrow streets and grand mansions of part of the Marais.

Fourth One of the most beautiful in Paris, with the eastern half of the Île de la Cité, Île St Louis, the major part of the Marais, the Tour St Jacques and Beaubourg (Georges Pompidou Centre).

Fifth Lively and entertaining, with the Latin Quarter, Roman and medieval Paris, and masses of students around the Sorbonne.

Sixth Vibrant street life with really good shopping and eating, around Boulevard Saint-Michel and Saint-Germain-des-Prés.

Seventh Monumental and grandiose, with the Eiffel Tower, the Hôtel des Invalides with its five museums and Napoleon's tomb, and the Assemblée Nationale.

Eighth Rich and glamorous, home of haute couture, the area round the Champs Elysées and Rue du Faubourg-St-Honoré.

Ninth The greatest concentration of hotels in Paris, best for affordable shopping and night life, from the department stores of the Grands Boulevards to the Pigalle cabarets.

Tenth The Gare du Nord and the Gare de l'Est, the Canal St Martin. A lot of red lights, working girls and boys.

Eleventh The Bastille, birthplace of the revolution, now young and somewhat trendy.

Twelfth Heading off the map into the Bois de Vincennes with its lakes and zoo.

BIRD'S EYE PARIS

Where to get up high and see the views:
Tour Montparnasse, page 93.
Eiffel Tower, page 77.
La Grande Arche de La Défense, page 98.
Basilique du Sacré Cœur, page 53.
Tower of Notre Dame Cathedral, page 33.
Arc de Triomphe, page 72.
Samaritaine roof terrace, page 39.
Georges Pompidou Centre roof terrace, page 42.

Thirteenth Rather ugly modern Chinese and
Vietnamese quarter with many good, cheap Chinese
restaurants.

Fourteenth Best seen from underground, home to the
Catacombs and the Montparnasse Cemetery.

Fifteenth Montparnasse, once home to artists and
musicians and still a place of excess, with Tour
Montparnasse, the highest tower in Paris, and rue
Vaugirard – the longest street in the city (4360m
[2³/₄ miles]).

Sixteenth Très chic, très snob . . . Residential area
around the Palais de Chaillot, with tall, elegant houses,
inhabited by tall, elegant people, on long, elegant streets.

Seventeenth The Palais des Congrès. A residential area.

Eighteenth Tourist heaven, home of Montmartre, with
charming bistros, bad artists and excellent views.

Nineteenth The Parc de la Villette – revitalized as a
techno-beacon with the Cité des Sciences et de
l'Industrie.

Twentieth A non-area, surrounding the Père Lachaise
Cemetery.

> **THE FRENCH**
>
> *'The French character is
> indeed a character, stampt
> upon them from without.
> Their profoundest thoughts
> are bon mots. They are the
> only nation that ever existed,
> in which a government can
> be hissed off the stage like a
> bad play, and in which its fall
> excites less consternation,
> than the violation of a
> fashion in dress.'*
> J. C. and A. Hare, *Guesses
> at Truth*, 1847.

Below: *Wrought-iron
balconies in Montmartre
have changed little since
the artists made this
quarter their own in
the 19th century.*

GROWTH OF A CITY

1180–1223 King Philippe-Auguste builds a city wall and the Louvre fortress.
1364 Charles V builds new city wall and the Bastille fortress.
1546–59 The first quays along the river and first street lights installed.
1605 Development of the Marais begins.
1627 Île St Louis developed as a residential district.
1760 Building of Place de la Concorde, the Panthéon and Ecole Militaire.
1837 First railway line in France opens between Paris and St-Germain-en-Laye.
1852–70 Baron Haussmann totally redesigns and rebuilds the city (*see* page 8).
1900 First metro line opened.
1969 Food market moves to Rungis and Les Halles redeveloped.
1974 The Boulevard Périphérique and Tour Montparnasse completed.

HISTORY IN BRIEF

The history of Paris is one of death from famine and disease amongst the poor, of ostentatious consumption amongst the rich, all stained by the blood of war and siege, riot and revolution. The city has been invaded or besieged by the Romans, Alemanni, Franks, Huns, Vikings, English and, several times, the Germans.

The gaps between were filled by home-grown violence, directed usually at an autocratic monarchy with little grasp of the real world. Almost all the turmoil that spread throughout France began with the Paris mob, who started not only the 1789 revolution but many others as well. As far back as 1270 and 1277, Parisians

Right: *The history of Paris is to a great extent the history of France, and the figure of the Emperor Napoleon towers over both. His exploits are commemorated throughout the city, and he is buried impressively in Les Invalides.*

held their first recorded general strikes, which resulted in King Louis IX setting up the first municipal council, run by the guilds. In 1356 they stormed the palace and forced the Dauphin to grant a degree of parliamentary democracy – only for it to be revoked later the same year. The 19th century saw revolutions in 1830, 1848 and 1871; in the 20th century came the 'Student Revolt' of May 1968, which spread into many other strata of society and even across French borders.

Important Dates

c300BC Celtic Gaul Parisii tribe settle on the islands.

52BC Julius Caesar's troops defeat the Gauls, who destroy the city. By the 1st century AD, the Romans have built a small but thriving new city, Lutetia.

AD256–80 First Barbarian invasions. City almost destroyed by Franks and Alemanni.

c261 St Denis, first Bishop of Lutetia, is martyred.

360 City name changed to Paris.

451 St Geneviève leads triumphant defence of Paris against Attila the Hun, and becomes its patron saint after her death in 509 (*see* page 91).

508 Frankish king, Clovis, defeats Romans. Paris becomes capital of the Christian Merovingian empire.

8th–9th century Paris becomes a backwater as Charlemagne moves his capital to Aix-la-Chapelle. Empire attacked by Normans (Vikings) in 845, 846 and 861.

885 Eudes, Count of Paris, repulses Norman siege and his heirs become the most powerful of the French lords.

987 Hugues Capet, is declared King of France, founding the Capetian dynasty.

1163 Notre Dame begun.

1183 Opening of permanent food market in Les Halles.

1215 The University of Paris given official recognition.

1253 Sorbonne University founded.

1302 First meeting of the Estates General, France's closest answer to a parliament, made up of representatives of the nobility, clergy and bourgeoisie.

c1310 Establishment of the Parlement de Paris as a judicial court.

1337 The Hundred Years War against England begins.

1348 Plague outbreak kills over a third of the population.

1356 King Jean II is captured by the English, leaving France in anarchy.

1356 The Provost, Etienne Marcel, storms the palace with a mob, forcing the Dauphin, the future King Charles V, to grant parliamentary democracy. Marcel is later killed,

PARIS FIRSTS

1534 St Ignatius Loyola founds the Society of Jesus (Jesuits) on Montmartre.

1783 First manned ascent in hot air balloon by Pilatre de Rozier and the Marquis d'Arlandes.

1818 Daguerre and Niepce invent photography.

1885 Louis Pasteur invents the principles of inoculation with rabies vaccine.

1895 Auguste and Louis Lumière invent the ciné camera and show the world's first movie. They also invent colour photography.

1898 Pierre and Marie Curie discover radium.

1983 Luc Montagnier isolates the AIDS virus.

and all democratic rights are revoked.

1420 English king, Henry V, occupies Paris and claims the throne of France.

1429 Unsuccessful siege, led by Joan of Arc.

1437 Charles VII recaptures an anarchic and virtually bankrupt Paris.

1528 François I moves from the Marais into the Louvre, which becomes a royal palace.

1562–98 The Wars of Religion between Catholics and Huguenots split France. Catherine de Medici arranges a truce, gathers Huguenot leaders in Paris and massacres them (1572), together with over 10,000 other Protestants nationwide. War ends when Protestant king Henry IV (of Navarre) besieges Paris, converts to Catholicism to claim the throne, then signs the Edict of Nantes, guaranteeing freedom of worship.

1610–42 Reign of Louis XIII, controlled by Cardinal Richelieu, becomes a golden age of bourgeois prosperity and efficiency for the city.

1643–1715 Reign of Louis XIV, the megalomaniac 'Sun King', who nearly bankrupts the country by his lavish lifestyle, creates unworkably detailed laws, sets up a highly unpopular network of spies and overtaxes everyone. At the same time, his reign is a triumph of luscious, frothy music, art and theatre.

1648–60 Several small-scale rebellions against the king, including the Fronde.

1682 Entire court, including 10,000 aristocratic hangers-on, moves to Versailles.

1685 Louis XIV revokes the Edict of Nantes.

1789 Start of the French Revolution (*see* page 15).

1804 Napoleon crowns himself Emperor in Notre Dame.

1814 Napoleon is exiled to Elba. Elderly Louis XVIII is restored to the throne.

1815 After his escape, Napoleon marches back to Paris. He is defeated for the last time at Waterloo and is exiled to St Helena, where he dies in 1821.

1830 A three-day revolution topples ineffective Charles X, replacing him by a distant relative, Louis-Philippe.

1832 19,000 Parisians die in cholera epidemic.

1848 Revolution of Contempt leads to the Second Republic with Napoleon's nephew, Louis-Napoleon, elected president.

1851 Louis-Napoleon declares himself Emperor Napoleon III. Start of Second Empire.

1852–70 Haussmann virtually rebuilds Paris (*see* page 8).

1870–71 The Franco–Prussian War. Napoleon is captured; radicals take over the Assemblée Nationale, declaring a Third Republic, based at Versailles. Paris is besieged by Germans; Parisians form themselves into a Committee of National Defence. They hold off the siege, but the Assemblée Nationale surrenders and Germans march into Paris. In the aftermath the committee resists attempts to disarm it and forms the Paris Commune, which is eventually controlled after six weeks of bloody fighting with French government troops, leaving over 20,000 dead, another 25,000 imprisoned and untold damage to the city. Paris loses any form of real self-government for the next 106 years.

1914 Paris escapes invasion during World War I after Battle of the Marne, as Paris taxi

CALENDAR OF THE REVOLUTION

1784 The Farmers-General (tax-gatherers) persuade Louis XVI to build a new wall round an already distressed city, to help them collect entry tolls.

1789 With the country falling to pieces, Louis is persuaded to call the Estates General for the first time since 1614.

5 May The Estates convene at Versailles.

17 June The commons declare themselves a National Assembly and promise to give France a constitution before they stand down.

12 July Crowds attack the toll booths on the Farmers Wall.

14 July A mob storms the Bastille. Lafayette forms the Paris militia and designs the tricolour – with royal white and the red and blue of Paris.

November All church property is confiscated.

1790 Nobles and clergy renounce all their privileges.

1791 Royal family captured while attempting to escape Paris, and held as prisoners in the Tuileries.

10 August 1792 Crowds take the Louvre and the hardline Commune overthrows the relatively moderate government.

22 September A new *Convention Nationale* is elected and proclaims a Republic.

21 January 1793 Execution of Louis XVI ends 805 years of the monarchy. The severed head is displayed to the crowd.

2 June Communards overthrow the Convention and arrest moderate Girondins.

September Start of the Terror, led by Marat and Robespierre. 2600 people sent to the Guillotine.

27 July 1794 Robespierre himself is executed, ending the Terror. Power moves to a new five-man *Directoire*.

1799 Napoleon Bonaparte stages a successful coup, enticing the whole government to St Cloud for their protection and arresting them.

1804 Napoleon declares himself Emperor.

drivers rally to drive reserve troops to the front.

1919 Versailles Treaty ends World War I.

June 1940 Government flees, leaving Paris to be occupied by Nazis.

August 1944 Paris liberated. Allies hold back and the Free French under Leclerc lead the triumphant entry. De Gaulle arrives two days later.

May 1968 Student riots spread across the country.

1977 Jacques Chirac is elected first mayor of Paris since 1871.

1989 Huge bicentenary of the Revolution celebrations.

1998 France proudly hosts, and wins, the soccer World Cup.

May 2001 Socialist Bertrand Delanoë becomes Paris' (and a European capital's) first openly gay mayor.

Below: *The names of those who died in the three-day revolution of July 1830 are inscribed on the July Column in the Place de la Bastille.*

GOVERNMENT AND ECONOMY

Paris has been the capital of France for 2000 years and the politics of city and state are inexorably entwined. France is a republic, led by an executive President, who is elected for five years and governs with the aid of a Prime Minister and cabinet. There are two houses of parliament; the law-making *Assemblée Nationale*, elected for five years, and the *Sénat*, elected for nine years, with advisory powers only.

Internally, however, power in France is largely devolved to the provinces, with the country split into 22 regions, 96 départements and 36,532 communes. Each Paris arrondissement has its own council and adminis-tration, and the city as a whole is a département, under the auspices of the *Conseil de Paris*.

Paris Politics

Much of the violence and bloodshed in French history stems from the determination of Parisians to have greater freedom of self-government. The power of the mob has ebbed and flowed over the centuries and most rulers have feared its wrath, but the succession of revolutions in 1789, 1830 and 1848, followed by the 1871 Commune, became too much to take. All semblance of local government was dismantled and the city was brought under direct state control. It was 106 years

Right: *The understated chic of the fashion house Yves St Laurent prêt-à-porter, on the Rive Gauche.*

before Paris finally regained a mayor in 1977, with the outspoken and politically ambitious Jacques Chirac. Almost from the moment he took office the struggle for control began again, but this time with monuments as weapons. The city became a giant Lego set as President and Mayor battled to create its most impressive building and most spectacular celebration.

Above: *A trip on a tour boat under the bridges of Paris is an ideal way to view the city's sights.*

Economy

On the whole, all this rivalry has been good for the development of infrastructure. The city has been carefully restored, is well kempt and efficiently run – and it has some of the most exciting and innovative modern architecture in Europe. There has also been a massive boom in tourism, which is now the city's main money-spinner. There are some other money-making industries, most notably fashion, with the couturier houses as loss-leaders and spin-offs such as ready-to-wear and perfume making the money, while the surrounding Île de France is heavily industrial. On the whole, however, central Paris feeds on itself and the rest of the country – a charming showcase of society and government, the arts and media.

CHIRAC

Born in 1932, Jacques René Chirac was elected to the Assemblée Nationale in 1967 and became Prime Minister in 1974. Two years later he resigned to form a breakaway Gaullist party. In 1977 he became Mayor of Paris, a position he held until 1995. He was unsuccessful in his bid for the Presidency in 1981. Ever optimistic, however, he stood again for the 1995 presidential election and this time was successful in his challenge. He was re-elected in May 2002.

Above: *Exclusive shops line the Place Vendôme.*

THE PEOPLE

Everyone knows the clichés – Parisians are unwelcoming and haughty, intellectually pretentious, appalling drivers and terrible snobs. Some are, of course. Certain types do still exist: the well-bred *haute bourgeoisie*, with their drawl and old-fashioned chic; the old-style working class, who survive in small residential pockets in the city and can be seen buying food in the markets every day. However, the city is changing. Many people living in Paris today are immigrants, not only from provincial France, but from all over Europe, Africa and Asia. About the only truism left is that all Parisians *know* Paris is the centre of the civilized universe and barely recognize the existence of the rest of the world – except as a source of ingredients and for one month a year, during the August holiday, when they spill out of town *en masse* to the countryside and coast.

Religion

Although the church and state were formally separated in 1905, France is traditionally Catholic and most Parisians pay nominal service to the Church. Like most modern cities, few are devout and regular attendance at services is dropping. At the same time, the influx of North Africans has resulted in a growing Muslim population and there are also representatives of every other faith and cult somewhere in the city.

Lifestyle

Life in Paris is up-beat, fast-moving, exciting, invigorating, and totally exhausting. Parisians pride themselves on being sophisticated, highly educated and well read, on their broad-minded and tolerant attitude and their refusal to be shocked. They are enthusiastic

BALLOONING

In 1783 word reached Paris of the Montgolfier brothers' experiment. Paris went balloon-crazy. Two months later, physicist Jacques Charles released the city's first balloon, launching it from the Place des Victoires. Shortly after that, Pilatre de Rozier and the Marquis d'Arlandes made the first manned ascent, flying a distance of 100m (330ft) from the Château de Muette to the Butte-aux-Cailles.

theatre- and cinema-goers – egged on partly by the lamentable quality of French TV – are willing to discuss new ideas ad nauseam, and keep up a noble tradition of civil strife, strikes and demonstrations.

The city is young, and society driven by the wealthy and childfree. You see remarkably few small children around and few concessions are made to them. People are staying single longer and having families later and, with the improvements in public transport, there is a growing tendency for Parisians to move out to the suburbs when they start a family.

Image is all important, whether in clothes, accessories or the quality of the furniture. Even if the salon is a museum piece, the private rooms behind may well be scruffy. Fashion swings like a metronome, as people scurry towards the new trendy district or restaurant. In terms of clothes, street fashion is a very mixed bag and by no means all Parisians have chic, but the majority are probably making some sort of statement. There is a high level of cultural appreciation and Parisians enjoy discussing and philosophizing at length over innovation, especially in art and ideas. They do so, however, in an atmosphere that cherishes the style and decorative detail that has traditionally meant 'Paris' to the rest of the world.

ETIQUETTE

Life is becoming less formal now, but older people will still wait for permission before using a first name or the familiar '*tu*', and invitations into the home only come with a degree of familiarity. Everyone shakes hands on meeting, but the normal greeting amongst friends is *la bise* – two kisses in central Paris, four in the suburbs and three in many other parts of France.

Below: *Boules is more a national passion than a pastime.*

THE ARTS
Architecture

The early 13th-century foundation of Notre Dame (1163)
and the Sainte-Chapelle (1245) heralded in the great era
of Gothic architecture that seemed to spring fully fledged
and triumphant from the narrow, grimy streets of Paris.
It was such a success that the city largely ignored Italy's
return to classical elegance and only caught up with the
Renaissance in the late 16th century with the rebuilding
of the Louvre (1546–59) and the Place des Vosges
(1605–12). Even so, it scarcely paused for breath before
sweeping on to the Baroque, epitomized by the lavish
flamboyance of Versailles (1661–82), and an era

Opposite: *The tomb of
Voltaire, the leading
philosophical writer of
the 18th-century Enlight-
enment, in the Panthéon.*
Right: *The colonnade
in the courtyard of the
Palais Royal provides a
contrasting backdrop for
a modern steel sculpture
by Paul Bury.*

dominated by the architect Le Vau (1612–70), painter Le Brun (1619–90) and landscape gardener Le Nôtre (1613–1700). Variations on this gilded glamour remained popular right into the 20th century, with several destructive puritanical interludes.

The Napoleons added a new sombre tone to the streets with massive, Imperial neo-classical buildings such as the Arc de Triomphe (1806–14 and 1832–6). The Great Exhibitions (*see* page 83) brought in experimental triumphs in iron and glass, such as the Eiffel Tower (1889) and Art Nouveau Grand Palais and Pont Alexandre III (both 1896–1900). The post-war era has seen an exciting new boom in innovative design, with projects such as the Georges Pompidou Centre (1977), the Louvre Pyramid (1988), the Grande Arche de La Défense (1989), the Opéra Bastille (1989) and the Bibliothèque Nationale de France (1997).

Literature

The intellectuals, and pseudo-intellectuals, of Paris have long regarded ideas as entertainment and words as sexy, lionizing philosophers from Abélard in the 12th century (*see* page 51) to the 20th-century Existentialists.

In 1634, Cardinal Richelieu founded the *Académie Française*, with its closed membership and closed minds, that has stripped thousands of words from the French language in the name of purity, leaving it much the poorer. The real golden age of French literature began as a frippery, in the resplendent court of Louis XIV, where many bored, wealthy nobles needed constant entertaining to stop them plotting rebellion. The resultant outpouring of fine drama was headed by Molière (1622–73), whose acid comedies of manner

THE COMÉDIE-FRANÇAISE

France's first national theatre, the Comédie-Française, has the official title of Le Théâtre Français. It was founded in 1680 by Louis XIV and brought together two Paris theatre companies, the Hôtel de Bourgogne (itself an amalgamation of the Théâtre du Marais with Molière's own company, Illustre Théâtre) and the Théâtre Guénégaud. With a royal grant the company enjoyed a number of privileges, but they were abolished during the Revolution and the theatre disbanded. Later re-established, it was granted a decree by Napoleon in 1812. The company has performed the works of all the great French dramatists, notably the plays of Corneille, Molière and Racine.

delighted the very people they satirized; and Corneille (1606–84) and Racine (1639–99), whose broad range of poetic tragedy and comedy is ranked alongside Shakespeare.

Two authors dominate the 18th century: Voltaire (1694–1778), author of outspoken ironic novels and short stories; and Beaumarchais (1732–99), whose works, *The Barber of Seville* and *The Marriage of Figaro*, were transformed into Mozart's finest operas. Other philosophical writers of the time were Rousseau (1712–78), whose work *Emile* opened up the debate on education; and Diderot (1713–84), whose Encyclopedia brought together numerous contributors in an attempt to set down a rational explanation for the universe. The 19th century saw a new flowering of literary genius amongst the city's novelists and poets, including the flamboyant Balzac (1799–1850); the romantics – Victor Hugo (1802–85), George Sand (1804–76), and Gustave Flaubert (1821–80); tragic Baudelaire (1821–67); the dry, moralist Emile Zola (1840–1902) and, introspective Marcel Proust (1871–1922).

In the 1920s and 30s numerous British and American authors, including Henry Miller, Ernest Hemingway, Gertrude Stein and George Orwell, headed for the Paris cafés. Depression and war interrupted the flow of ideas and alcohol, but both were revived in the 1950s with the advent of the Existentialists Jean-Paul Sartre, Simone de Beauvoir and Albert Camus, who made their home from home in Les Deux Magots Café in St-Germain.

Since then, the banner has been taken up by some-what esoteric authors such as Alain Robbe-Grillet and Nathalie Sarraute, but Paris is still waiting for a new flowering of talent that will grip the world.

OVER COFFEE

Café society flourished in 18th-century Paris. The cafés were places to meet friends, drink coffee and discuss politics or literature. Perhaps the most famous of them all was the Café Procope at no. 13 rue de l'Ancienne-Comédie. Here the *philosophes* would gather to debate at leisure. Voltaire was a frequent visitor and it is said that Diderot and d'Alembert first thought up the idea for their Encyclopedia here.

Music

Astonishingly, in spite of the superb Conservatoire de Paris and Opéra, Paris had little influence on music until the mid-19th century, mainly producing only frothy entertainment, with some honourable exceptions such as Lully (1632–87) and Gluck (1714–87), both of whom were foreign. Parisian Berlioz (1803–69) was forced to work abroad. As with the other arts, Parisian music reached its zenith in the 19th century when composers such as Rossini (1782–1868), Chopin (1810–49), Liszt (1811–86), Wagner (1813–83), Offenbach (1819–80), César Franck (1822–90), Saint-Saëns (1835–1921), Fauré (1845–1924), Debussy (1862–1918) and Ravel (1875–1937) flocked into the city, along with Diaghilev's Russian ballet. At the same time popular nightlife was becoming increasingly important. Possibly the city's greatest home-grown contribution has been to cabaret, sparked by the glamorous, high-kicking chorus line of the can-can (1830, to music by Offenbach), eventually producing singers such as Maurice Chevalier and Edith Piaf, and show-casing the great American Josephine Baker and German Marlene Dietrich.

Above: *The famous French mime artist, Marcel Marceau. The art of mime thrives in Paris and street performers enliven the areas around Montmartre and Beaubourg.*

Opposite: *The Polish-born composer Chopin spent much of his life in Paris and is buried in Père-Lachaise cemetery.*

Painting and Sculpture

In the Middle Ages the finest Parisian art was in the stones, glorious stained glass, exquisite reliquaries and illuminated manuscripts of the churches. Secular work was confined largely to furniture and Gobelin tapestries which doubled as central heating. However, during his unsuccessful wars in Italy, François I (1494–1547) discovered the High Renaissance, returning to Paris with Leonardo da Vinci and carts piled high with fine art. His

THE IMPRESSIONISTS

The Impressionist painters delighted in conveying light and atmosphere, enjoying colour for its own sake. As a group of artists they are individual in style, but are linked by their interest in painting directly from nature and in developing the theories of harmonious and complementary colour. Inspired by Manet's exhibition of 1863 (*see page 82*) and disillusioned with the established academic attitude to art, they held their first joint exhibition in 1874. The name came from Monet's painting *Impression: Sunrise* and was used as an umbrella term by a critic to deride the group. There were eight Impressionist exhibitions in all and the painters exhibiting in each varied, though those involved included Monet, Renoir, Sisley, Pissarro, Cézanne, Degas and Morisot.

successors grasped the idea but not the quality and Parisian art settled back into fluffy decoration, propagandist statues and second-rate portraits, with delightful exceptions such as the delicate and romantic works of Watteau (1684–1721), Boucher (1703–70) and Fragonard (1732–1806).

Revolution and the 19th century saw a complete change, as artists such as Corot (1796–1875) and Delacroix (1799–1863) took to the streets, painting the scenes around them and infusing their work with a new depth while maintaining a deft touch with exquisite use of light and richness of colour. They opened a floodgate of new ideas and experimentation that has changed the course of artistic history.

Paris now became home to the greatest gathering of artistic talent since Renaissance Florence as artists flocked to the city from all over France. The roll-call is stupendous – Pissarro (1830–1903), Manet (1832–83), Degas (1834–1917), Cézanne (1839–1906), Rodin (1840–1917), Monet (1840–1926), Renoir (1841–1919), Henri Rousseau (1844–1910), Gauguin (1848–1903), Van Gogh (1853–90), Seurat (1859–91) and Toulouse-Lautrec (1864–1901), to name but a few. Ideas flourished, with

Right: *Parisians enjoy sculpture in the open air. This bronze statue of a female nude is in the Jardin des Tuileries.*

Left: *Local artists in the Place du Tertre, Montmartre.*

Impressionism, Pointillism, Fauvism and Expressionism. Paris rejected them all, however, and most of these great artists lived in abject poverty throughout their lives.

With the new century came Cubism and Surrealism and a new crop of superb artists, including Matisse (1869–1954), Mondrian (1872–1945), Epstein (1880–1959), Léger (1881–1955), Picasso (1881–1973), Braques (1882–1963), Utrillo (1883–1955), Modigliani (1884–1920), Chagall (1887–1985), Ernst (1891–1976) and Miró (1893–1983). Until the outbreak of World War II it became crucial for any serious artist to study in Paris. Today the city is still actively sponsoring new work, but the artistic community is more fragmented and, thanks to air travel, we are unlikely ever again to see such a concentration of talent in one city.

CINEMA

Since Auguste and Louis Lumière opened the world's first cinema in Paris in 1895, the city has remained the centre of a small but steady French film industry that has produced several of the world's finest film-makers, including Jean Renoir (son of the painter), Abel Gance, Marcel Pagnol, Jean Cocteau, Jacques Tati, François Truffaut, Jean-Luc Goddard and Louis Malle, and some of the world's favourite stars, such as Maurice Chevalier, Charles Boyer, Jean-Paul Belmondo, Simone Signoret, Brigitte Bardot, Jeanne Moreau, Gérard Dépardieu, Catherine Deneuve and Alain Delon.

FOOD AND DRINK

Parisians appear obsessed by food. The city is a gastronome's heaven, the spiritual and physical home of haute cuisine, with possibly the greatest concentration of fine food in the world. However, all is not as rosy as it might seem in paradise.

The State of the Art

French eating habits are changing. Most women now work and simply do not have the time to cook long, luscious meals; busy, cholesterol-aware office workers are shunning the traditional three-course lunch in favour of a quick snack at their desk; and supermarkets are squeezing out many smaller shops. Everyday food is much simpler than before, with frozen and vacuum-packed ingredients common and a booming trade in ready-prepared meals. These are usually traditional dishes such as *cassoulet* or *coq au vin*, but global standbys, from pizza to burgers are becoming distressingly common.

All this change, tragically, has begun to filter through into the restaurants and cafés and you can no longer be assured of quality. There are still delightful traditional restaurants and chic new bistros with imaginative young chefs. But there are also many corner-cutting brasseries serving unimaginative, microwaved food, who rely on a flashy shopfront and gullible passing tourists to fill their coffers.

Below: *Take the weight off your feet, sip a drink and simply watch the world go by at a pavement café.*

The Internal Clock

A typical French breakfast is milky coffee or hot chocolate with a croissant or baguette and jam. Many hotels, used to international visitors, may add the choice of ham and cheese, fruit juice and yoghurt.

Lunch can be a simple snack or a full meal. Go early, as restaurants begin

35 **VINS FINS DESSERTS**

RUE DE PROVENCE

FRUITS SECS

FRUITS CONFITS

THÉS

MAGASIN SPÉCIAL de DESSERTS d'HIVER

FRUITS SECS pour COMPOTES

FABRIQUE DE CHOCOLATS **A LA MÈRE DE FAMILLE** FONDÉE EN 1761 CONFISERIE E DESSERTS

to fill up from 12:00 onwards. If on a limited budget, consider eating your main meal at midday as the fixed price lunch menus are excellent value, while a light snack, such as an omelette and salad, can be horribly expensive. Some places, however, also do a good value one-course *plat du jour*. Alternatively, the best option is to picnic. The key ingredients – bread, paté, cheese, sausage and fruit – are all easily available, as are bottled water, wine and cans of soda. Many delicatessens also sell ready-made salads, quiches, made-up sandwiches and pizza. Some parts of the parks are off limits, but there are plenty of benches and fountain steps, and the quays beside the Seine are excellent picnic spots.

Dinner begins surprisingly early, at about 19:00. Do not arrive much after 21:00 or everything will be full. Ideally, it is safer to reserve in advance. Eating after the theatre or opera is not easy, unless you go 'ethnic' or to the more bohemian areas of the Left Bank. Again, most

Above: *In many areas of Paris there are still traditional shops that sell wines, delicious honeys, jams and conserves, teas, chocolate and savoury delicacies.*

restaurants have a range of two- or three-course set menus at different prices, all of which are cheaper than the à la carte options. Some also include wine and coffee.

Bistro or Brasserie

The range and sheer number of restaurants in Paris is overwhelming. Choosing where to eat can be one of the greatest pleasures of your holiday (*see* Paris at a Glance, page 116). A few top restaurants are so famous that you have to book months in advance, and probably take out a large bank loan. For a good, relatively cheap meal, select an area, then wander the side streets, reading menu boards outside until you find one that makes you salivate. Avoid those with too long a menu. Food is likely to be fresher and cooked specially for you with only a limited number of dishes on offer. The 1st arrondissement, just behind the Louvre, has many excellent options at a higher price. For cheaper meals, the best hunting areas are Montmartre/Pigalle and the Latin Quarter.

The café/bar serves drinks, coffee and light snacks such as *croque-monsieur* (toasted ham and cheese sandwich) or *assiette anglaise* (assortment of salamis and cold meats) all day. It is always cheaper to stand at the bar than to sit at a table and it may be even more expensive to sit at one of the premium pavement tables.

Right: *Cheeses from every part of France are sold in the heart of the city.*

The brasserie originally started life as a beerhouse but has grown over the years into another form of eatery. Brasseries serve a basic menu of simple food such as *steak frites* (steak and chips), shellfish, omelettes, sausage *andouillette* (tripe sausage) and *choucroute garnie* (sauerkraut with meats) – and, of course, different beers. They serve food all day and usually have a reasonably priced set meal to keep you going.

The 'bistro' was named in 1917 by Russian emigrés (the word is Russian for 'quick'). Bistros began life as the Parisian fast-food joints, small, cheap and cheerful restaurants serving a limited menu of hearty, unpretentious food. In their present form, they are still small and cheerful, with a slightly more ambitious menu and wine list and, usually, with a bar attached.

Above: *The interior of this Art Nouveau café retains its decorative detail and recalls the atmosphere of the giddy, social 1890s.*

Ethnic Options

Most of the cheaper French restaurants tend to have remarkably similar menus. However, the city is also home to an amazing array of other ethnic cuisines, brought here by Russian and Polish refugees, immigrants from Greece and Italy, and former colonials from North Africa, the Caribbean and Vietnam. Alongside these establishments are Thai, Japanese and Indian restaurants and even English and Irish pubs. Many of these are excellent, offer extraordinarily good value, are one of few viable options for vegetarians and can be a welcome change from another *steak au poivre*.

2
The Islands

ÎLE DE LA CITÉ ★★★
(metro: Cité, Pont Neuf, St Michel)
The Conciergerie
Along the northern Quai de l'Horloge, the formidable **Conciergerie** began life as the 4th-century home of the Roman governor and 6th-century royal palace of Merovingian King Clovis. It remained the centre of government until 1358, after which the southern half, the **Palais de Justice**, became the home of parliament and the Supreme Court, while the northern half, the Conciergerie, housed the Concierge (Keeper of the Keys – a powerful politician whose duties included levying taxes) and the city prison. Amongst the earliest surviving buildings are the 13th-century Tour Bonbec (Babblers Tower), site of the torture chamber, and the Tour de l'Horloge, its public clock first installed in 1370.

Come the Revolution, the fortress entered its darkest and bloodiest period. In 1793–4 alone, during the worst days of the Terror, some 2700 people were imprisoned here on their way to the Guillotine, amongst them Queen Marie-Antoinette, Madame du Barry, Charlotte Corday (who stabbed Marat in his bath) and Citizens Danton and Robespierre. In a railed-off area, called the Rue de Paris, the prisoners of the Revolution were kept crowded together, sleeping on straw, being too poor to bribe their warders for better conditions. The guided tour takes you through several fine medieval halls, the kitchens, the executioner's apartments and the cells, including that of Marie-Antoinette.

PARIS

Seine

The Islands

Boulevard Peripherique

DON'T MISS

★★★ **The Cathedral of Notre Dame**
★★★ **The Sainte-Chapelle**
Two of the finest examples of Gothic architecture in the world.

Opposite: *The west (main) portal of the cathedral of Notre Dame shows the figure of Christ on its pier and sculptures representing the Last Judgment in the tympanum above.*

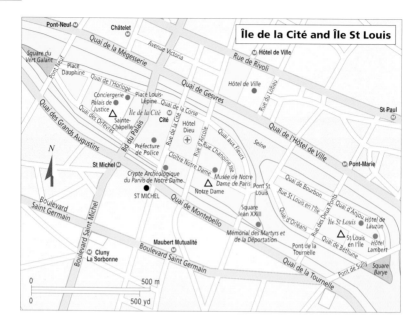

Île de la Cité and Île St Louis

Pont-Neuf · Châtelet · Avenue Victoria · Hôtel de Ville · Rue de Rivoli
Square du Vert Galant · Quai de la Mégesserie · Place Dauphine · Quai de l'Horloge · Quai de Gesvres · Hôtel de Ville · Rue du Lobau
Conciergerie · Place Louis-Lépine · Quai de la Corse · St Paul
Palais de Justice · Quai des Orfèvres · Île de la Cité · Cité · Hôtel Dieu · Quai de l'Hôtel de Ville
Sainte-Chapelle · Bd du Palais · Rue de la Cité · Rue d'Arcole · Rue Chanoine Sse · Quai aux Fleurs · Seine
Préfecture de Police · Cloître Notre Dame · Rue Chanoine Sse
St Michel · Pont-Marie
Crypte Archéologique du Parvis de Notre Dame · Musée de Notre Dame de Paris · Quai de Bourbon · Quai d'Anjou
ST MICHEL · Notre Dame · Pont St Louis · Rue St Louis en l'Île · Île St Louis · Hôtel de Lauzun
Quai de Montebello · Square Jean XXIII · Quai d'Orléans · Rue des Deux Ponts · St Louis en l'Île · Hôtel Lambert
Boulevard Saint Germain · Boulevard Saint Michel · Maubert Mutualité · Boulevard Saint Germain · Mémorial des Martyrs et de la Déportation · Pont de la Tournelle · Quai de Béthune · Pont de Sully · Square Barye
Cluny La Sorbonne · Quai de la Tournelle

N

0 ———— 500 m
0 ———— 500 yd

The Sainte-Chapelle ★★★

In the 19th century the Palais de Justice was rebuilt, along with the French legal system. Virtually hidden by its high walls is the gemlike Sainte-Chapelle, built in 1245–8 by architect Pierre de Montreuil for King Louis IX (1226–70) to house Christ's crown of thorns and other relics the king had retrieved from Venetian pawnbrokers. Some were lost during the Revolution, but those saved are now in Notre Dame, and the slender, filigree building is more museum than church, with Mass celebrated only on 10 May, feast of St Yves, patron saint of lawyers. At ground-floor level is the servants' chapel, its sumptuous paintwork a product of 19th-century restoration. The upper royal chapel, a soaring triumphant kaleidoscope of stained glass linked together by fragile, fluted columns, is without doubt one of the world's most glorious architectural achievements.

The scene of many royal weddings, it was here in 1396 that Richard II of England was betrothed to Isabella, daughter of Charles VI of France.

Below: *The lower chapel of the exquisite Sainte-Chapelle, used by the royal servants, is a masterpiece of vaulting.*

Cathedral of Notre Dame ★★★

The magnificent cathedral, another Gothic masterpiece, is the culmination of numerous temples to pagan Cernunnos, guardian of the underworld, Roman Jupiter, and several Christian churches. Built between 1163 and 1330, it is 130m (425ft) long, with 69m (223ft) towers. The spire, added by 19th-century restorer Viollet-le-Duc, along with the splendid gargoyles of the *Galerie des Chimières* and green copper roof statues, is 90m (300ft) high.

The superb early 13th-century west façade begins with three arches, dedicated to the Virgin (left), St Anne (right), and the Last Judgment (centre). Above is the *Galerie des Rois d'Israel*, ancestors of Christ, and above that are Adam and Eve and the Virgin, surrounded by angels. It is possible to climb the 387 steps of the North Tower to see the bells, roofs, gargoyles and superb views over Paris.

There are three rose windows, each 13m (43ft) in diameter. The oldest and finest, in the north transept, was donated by St Louis in the 13th century and depicts Old Testament figures surrounding the Virgin. The south

Above: *Notre Dame's rose windows have inspired generations of craftsmen.*

GLORIOUS GLASS

The Sainte-Chapelle has nearly 1500m² (16,000 sq ft) of stained glass in 15 massive windows containing 1100 separate scenes. Of these, about 750 are 13th-century originals, the oldest in Paris. The others are superb 19th-century copies. The rose window, telling the story of Revelations, was added by Charles VIII in 1485. Together, they make up a pictorial bible. To read them, start in the lower left-hand corner and read left to right, travelling upwards.

Above: *A view of Notre Dame from the Square Jean XXIII shows the distinctive flying buttresses.*
Below: *The Wallace fountain in the Rue Lépine on the Île de la Cité.*

rose, which is heavily restored, is dedicated to the New Testament, surrounding Christ in Majesty. The view of the west window, over the main door, is partially blocked by the magnificent organ, one of the largest in the world, with 108 stops and 7800 pipes.

Inside, tiny side chapels, many of them sponsored by medieval guilds, surround the towering nave. Through the centre a magnificent 14th-century carved screen, depicting the Nativity (north) and Resurrection (south), separates the ambulatory from the choir. The choir itself was rebuilt in 1723, honouring a vow made by Louis XIII. At the top is a beautiful Pietà by Nicolas Coustou, flanked by marble Louis XIII and XIV. A door in the southeast wall opposite leads to the Treasury, a rich collection of gold and silver reliquaries, ivory figures, books and historical memorabilia.

Parvis du Notre Dame

The original square was a quarter of the size of today's vast, echoing Parvis du Notre Dame, created by Baron Haussmann in the mid-19th century (*see page 8*). A brass star set into the pavement just in front of Notre Dame marks **Point Zéro**, the exact point from which all distances in France are measured. On the north side, the massive **Hôtel Dieu** has been the city's main hospital since AD660; to the west is the **Préfecture de Police**, site of a ferocious four-day battle between the police and German soldiers during the 1944 liberation of Paris.

In 1965 developers building a car park under the Parvis found a fascinating slice of history, with Roman and medieval walls and streets, the Merovingian cathedral and an 18th-century Foundlings Hospital. These are now preserved in the **Crypte Archéologique du Parvis de Notre Dame**, a beautifully presented underground museum that makes perfect sense of the maze of broken walls.

Other Sights

The charming **Place Dauphine** and the green and peaceful **Square du Vert Galant** named 'jolly rogue' after the rollicking, womanizing king, Henry IV (of Navarre) once formed a separate islet, the Île de Juif, used for burning Jews and witches, amongst them the Templar Grand Master, Jacques de Molay. The original equestrian statue of Henry IV was melted during the Revolution. This copy was made from the toppled statue of Napoleon which once graced the Vendôme Column. Nearby, the **Pont Neuf** is the oldest surviving bridge in Paris, opened in 1607 and, until the Revolution, the fashionable place to stroll and be seen.

A cool green daily flower market in **Place Louis-Lépine** gives way to a chattering bird market on Sundays. Behind the cathedral are a small museum dedicated to its history, the **Musée de Notre Dame de Paris**, *10 rue du Cloître Notre Dame, 4th*, and the little tree-lined **Square Jean XXIII**, site of the Bishop's Palace (destroyed by rioters in 1831), which offers superb views of the gloriously complex flying buttresses and statues which adorn the outside of the cathedral.

The eastern tip of the island is dedicated to the simple, but highly emotive modern **Mémorial des Martyrs et de la Déportation**, dedicated to the 200,000 Frenchmen and women – including 76,000 Jews – who died in Nazi labour and concentration camps during World War II.

> **A TURBULENT LIFE**
>
> Over the years, Notre Dame has seen the coronations of Henry VI of England (1430) and Napoleon Bonaparte (1804); thanksgiving services to celebrate the liberation of Paris from the English (1437) and the Germans (1944). During the Revolution it was badly damaged, renamed the Temple of Reason, with a local ballerina as goddess, and only narrowly escaped demolition thanks to the timely publication of Victor Hugo's novel, *The Hunchback of Notre Dame* (1831). It was further damaged in 1871 when Communards set it ablaze, changed their minds, but mistaking the Gallery of Kings of Israel and Judea on the façade for Kings of France, settled for lopping their heads off.

Below: *The Pont Neuf, the oldest bridge in Paris, connects the Île de la Cité with both banks of the Seine.*

ÎLE ST LOUIS WALK

Start at metro Pont Marie. Cross the bridge and turn left onto Quai d'Anjou. Turn right past Square Barye, and right again onto Quai de Béthune. Take the first right, then first left onto Rue St Louis en l'Ile. At Rue des Deux Ponts, turn left, then right onto Quai d'Orléans. Follow this round to the Pont St Louis, then turn right onto Rue St Louis en l'Ile. Back at Rue des Deux Ponts, turn left for Pont Marie and the metro.

ST LOUIS

Born in 1214, King Louis IX succeeded to the throne at the age of 12. The years of regency under his mother led to rebellion among the feudal nobility, but once he had taken over the government Louis established legal and administrative reforms and promoted wider education. He fought in the Crusades, brought back many holy relics to France, and was responsible for the building of Sainte-Chapelle and the Sorbonne. Louis is revered for his sense of justice and his personal piety and religious devotion. He died in Tunis in 1270 from the plague.

ÎLE ST LOUIS **
(metro: Pont Marie, Cité, Sully Morland)

Extraordinarily, Île St Louis was virtually uninhabited until the 17th century, used only for laundry, fishing and grazing. Charles V (1338–80) dug a defensive canal along the line of modern Rue Poulletier, creating two small islands, Île Notre Dame and Île aux Vaches. In 1627, as building boomed in the nearby Marais, an architect, Christophe Marie, and two financiers, Poulletier and le Regrattier, obtained a 60-year lease, permission to rejoin the two islands and the rights to sell building land. They laid out the basic grid of streets, surrounded the island by tree-lined quays and encouraged the noble and wealthy to buy. The resulting residential area has great elegance, enormous charm, a permanent population of around 6000, and feels as peaceful as a Sunday afternoon in the park.

There are few real sights. Instead, amble through the narrow streets and round the tranquil quays shaded by rustling poplar trees, breathe in the atmosphere and admire the detail on the fine classical *hôtels particuliers* (private mansions). Many of the houses have plaques that name their illustrious inhabitants, who include bankers, politicians, artists, sculptors, writers and poets. The **Quais de Bourbon** and **d'Anjou**, were originally *the* place to live. A plain façade hides the lusciously decorative interior of the **Hôtel de Lauzun**, *17, quai d'Anjou, 4th* (open weekends). Built in 1657 for a financier who was sent to prison before he could move in, the house is named after the Duke of Lauzun, who commanded the French at the Battle of the Boyne. Among the artists involved in its decoration were Le Brun, Le Sueur and Bourdon. Gautier, Baudelaire, Rilke, Sickert and Wagner all lived here, while in the 1840s it became home to the popular *Club des Haschischins* (Hashish Eaters' Club), run by a famous prostitute, Aglaë-Apollonie Sabatier. The cartoonist Daumier lived at no. 9 on the Quai d'Anjou. At the foot of the island is a peaceful little park, the **Square Barye**, named after another local inhabitant, an animal sculptor.

The southern **Quais d'Orléans** and **de Béthune** are now the more fashionable addresses. The Quai d'Orléans offers fine views over the flying buttresses of Notre Dame, and Landowski's elongated 1928 statue of St Geneviève (*see* page 91) on the **Pont de la Tournelle**. At no. 6 are the Polish Library and the **Musée Adam-Mickiewicz**, with exhibits on Chopin and Mickiewicz, founder of the Polish Romantic movement.

Through the centre runs the main commercial **Rue St Louis en l'Île**. Halfway along, the baroque **Church of St Louis en l'Île** (1656–1725) was designed by Le Vau. It has an elaborately gilded interior, a striking iron clock and an extraordinary spire, pierced by ovals, built in 1765 to replace the original which was burnt by lightning. Classical music concerts are regularly held here.

Below: *The Quai de Béthune on the Île St Louis offers a relaxed walk by the river.*

Le Vau also built the **Hôtel Lambert** at no. 2 *Rue St Louis en l'Île*, which later became the home of Voltaire and Mme du Châtelet.

No. 51, the delightful Rococo **Hôtel Chenizot**, was the home of Theresia Cabarrus in the 1790s. Nicknamed *Notre Dame de Thermidor*, she had eleven illegitimate children and was said to have slept with virtually the entire Revolutionary government. No. 31 is the home of **Berthillon**, whose marvellous ice cream is a Parisian institution. The **Pont St Louis**, across to the Île de la Cité, is the ninth on the site; the site was cursed by Gypsies in 1472 and the first bridge collapsed the day it was opened in 1634, drowning 20 people.

3
Beaubourg, Les Halles, the Marais and Bastille

THE RIVER

If the Île de la Cité was the heart of royal and religious Paris, the right bank was undoubtedly the commercial centre. **La Samaritaine**, *19 rue de la Monnaie, 1st (metro: Pont Neuf)*, was opened in 1869 by a successful local merchant, Ernest Cognac, and named after a statue which stood under the arches of the Pont Neuf (*see page 35*). Today, it is one of the largest department stores in the city, with a superb Art Nouveau staircase and rooftop café which offers possibly the finest view in Paris.

The **Place du Louvre** *(metro: Louvre, Pont Neuf)* was once the headquarters of the Roman general, Labienus. The church of **St Germain l'Auxerrois**, first built in the 6th century, was fortified by the Normans and rebuilt as a collegiate church in 1025. From the 14th to the 19th century it became the royal chapel, and during the Revolution it even did duty as a gunpowder factory, police station and granary. In 1572 its bell was rung to mark the start of the St Bartholomew's Day Massacre (*see page 14*). The free-standing 19th-century belfry next door has an infinitely superior carillon of 38 bells, with regular recitals.

The **Place du Châtelet** stands on the site of a notoriously sinister medieval prison; underneath it is the world's largest metro station *(Châtelet-Les Halles)*. Just to the north is the beautiful 16th-century **Tour St Jacques**. This 52m (171ft) belfry is all that remains of the Eglise de St Jacques de la Boucherie, built by the Butchers' Guild at the official starting point of the pilgrim route to Santiago de Compostela in Spain.

PARIS

Seine

Beauborg

Boulevard Périphérique

DON'T MISS

*** Centre Georges Pompidou: France's national gallery of modern art in a mould-breaking building.
*** The Marais: walk the streets and alleys of this delightful old quarter and visit the Place des Vosges, the Musée Picasso and the Musée Carnavalet.

Opposite: *One of Niki de Saint-Phalle's colourful water sculptures at the Place Igor Stravinsky.*

STRIKES, GIBBETS AND BONFIRES

Until Baron Haussmann changed its name, the peaceful Place de l'Hôtel de Ville was called the Place de Grève. It was the traditional place to find work; 'to do the grève' meant to be out of work. Gradually, the word came to be used for a strike.

It was also a place of execution, with regular public beheadings, hangings and burnings. In 1793, at the start of the Terror, the Guillotine was moved here. Over the next 18 months, it became a human abattoir, drenched with the blood of 2600 victims. Robespierre, the architect of the bloodshed, was arrested here in 1794 and guillotined.

Municipal government in Paris has been centred on the **Place de l'Hôtel de Ville** since 1260. The first **Hôtel de Ville** proper was designed under François I, but only completed in the 17th century. It became the headquarters of the Paris Commune throughout the Revolution and the Third Republic was declared here in 1871. The following year the building was torched by irate Communards (*see* page 15). The current splendid building only dates from 1874–82, although the central panel is a copy of the Renaissance hôtel.

LES HALLES *

rue Berger, rue Rambuteau, 1st (metro: Châtelet-Les Halles)

Les Halles opened for business in about 1110. By 1183 Philippe-Auguste had commissioned the first permanent market hall and was collecting rent and tax from an ever-growing number of stall holders selling everything from offal to gold lace. In 1851 Victor Baltard designed a new expandable hall of glass and green iron 'umbrellas'. In

1969 the fruit and vegetable market moved to hygienic, high-tech premises in the southern suburbs of Rungis. By 1977 only a few street names were left to mark its passing, although the trendy have continued to come here to eat pigs' trotters and onion soup after the clubs close.

By 1979 a mushroom-topped modern complex sprouted from the gaping hole. Largely underground, it is mainly a busy, cavernous but uninspiring shopping mall with a huge cinema complex, swimming pool and restaurants.

On the whole, the large park on the roof is the best bit of the new complex. Broken into distinct areas by canopied walkways and pavilions, it has a fine children's playground and several interesting

Beaubourg, Les Halles, The Marais and Bastille

1. Centre Georges Pompidou
2. Fontaine des Innocents
3. Hôtel de Ville
4. Musée Carnavalet
5. Musée Cognacq-Jay
6. Musée des Arts et Métiers
7. Musée Picasso
8. Place des Vosges
9. Place Igor Stravinsky
10. Viaduc des Arts
11. Bibliothèque Nationale de France
12. Opéra Bastille
13. Hôtel de Sully
14. Musée de la Serrure
15. Musée de l'Histoire de France
16. Musée d'Art et d'Histoire du Judaïsme
17. Musée de la Chasse et de la Nature
18. Eglise de St-Louis-St-Paul

modern sculptures. The western end is marked by the circular **Bourse du Commerce**, the former granary exchange, beside which is a free-standing column once used by Catherine de Medici and her astrologers (including Nostradamus) as a platform for plotting the stars.

The crowning glory, however, is the view of the vast **Eglise de St-Eustache**. The first 13th-century church was built by a merchant made wealthy by market concessions. The existing high Gothic church (1532–1640) was modelled on Notre Dame, with an oddly disparate neo-classical façade added in 1754–88. Here Cardinal Richelieu, Molière and Madame de Pompadour were baptised; Louis XIV made his first holy communion;

Opposite: *St-Eustache framed by the ironwork of the Jardin des Halles, created when the market moved out of town.*

Above: *With the Place Igor Stravinsky Paris celebrates the music of the Russian composer with joyful water sculptures.*

Lully was married; and Louis XIV's minister, Colbert, La Fontaine, Molière and Mirabeau had their funerals. St-Eustache also saw the premieres of Berlioz' *Te Deum* and Liszt's *Messe de Gran*.

To the east, the small **Square des Innocents** began life as a graveyard, enclosed in 1186. It is said that during the siege of 1590 food in Paris became so short that locals ground bones from the charnel-house for flour. In 1780 an estimated two million corpses were finally removed to the Catacombs (*see* page 94). Today, the square contains several fast-food joints, numerous buskers and the enchanting Renaissance **Fontaine des Innocents**, designed by Pierre Lescot and carved by Jean Goujon in 1549, and moved here in 1788.

MULTI-COLOURED SCAFFOLDING

The structure of the Pompidou Centre is made of fourteen 12.8m (43ft) porticoes, each with two steel pillars 50m (165ft) apart. These are filled with water for added weight and fire protection. Each of the five floors is a vast open space of 7500m² (80,000 sq ft) (the size of two football pitches). The technical shafts are all on the outside of the building. On the east side, those painted blue are for air-conditioning, green are for fluids (eg water), yellow are for electrical shafts and red are for communication (eg lifts and escalators). The vast white pipes on the roof are the air-cooling ducts.

BEAUBOURG ★★★
(metro: Hôtel de Ville/Châtelet-Les Halles)

In the 1960s the poverty-stricken and ironically named Beaubourg (beautiful village) was cleared. In its place, from 1972–7, President Georges Pompidou commissioned two architects, British Richard Rogers and Italian Renzo Piano, to create a globally renowned centre for the arts. The controversial, futuristic, inside-out **Centre Georges Pompidou**, *19 rue Beaubourg, 4th*, fostered a whole new wave of modern design.

Take the glassed-in escalator up to the 6th floor and work down. As you rise the view expands outwards, while at your feet people swarm in ever-changing patterns around the many buskers in the piazza. The 6th floor is used for major international exhibitions.

The superb permanent collection of the **Musée National d'Art Moderne** covers work from the beginning of the 20th century to the present day on the 4th and 5th floors. The painings are arranged chronologically but the greatest works, by artists such as Matisse, Picasso, Kandinsky and Léger, are easily accessible in the main gallery. Side galleries are devoted to individual artists or movements. The third, second and part of the first floors are taken up by the Bibliothèque Publique d'Information.

There are also performance spaces with regular lectures, live performances and films.

The south wall abuts **Place Igor Stravinsky**, where Niki de Saint-Phalle's brightly coloured water sculptures, dedicated to works by Stravinsky, create an

Left: *The innovative Georges Pompidou Centre has become a major cultural magnet with numerous exhibition areas as well as media resources of all kinds.*

Right: *Le Défenseur du Temps in the Quartier de l'Horloge hourly fights the age-old battle against the elements.*

atmosphere of perpetual carnival. Between are black metal mobiles by Jean Tinguely. Narrow Rue St Martin leads south past the flamboyant Gothic **Eglise de St-Merri** (1520–1612), formerly parish church of the moneylenders in the Rue des Lombards. Look for the small hermaphroditic demon above the door. The interior was heavily altered during the reign of Louis XV.

To the north of the Pompidou Centre, in the **Quartier de l'Horloge**, is Jacques Monastier's **Le Défenseur du Temps**, *rue Bernard-de-Clairvaux, 3rd*, a magnificent 4m (13ft) high public clock of polished brass. On the hour, the warrior has to fend off the earth (dragon), the air (phoenix) or the sea (crab), complete with thundering sound effects. At 12:00, 18:00 and 22:00 he manages to defeat all the creatures as they assault him together.

THE MARAIS ★★★
(metro: Saint-Paul/Chemin Vert)

The name 'Marais' means 'marsh' and until the 16th century no scheme to drain and develop the unhealthy swamp really succeeded. The Templars tried, but their 13th-century walled town did not survive the disbanding of the order in 1307. Philippe-Auguste included the district in his walled city and in 1358, after the mob invaded the Conciergerie, the future Charles V lived for a while in the now defunct Hôtel St Pol.

The place only really began to take off in the 17th century when Henry IV built the **Place des Vosges** in 1605. Known originally as the Place Royale, it was renamed by Napoleon in 1800 after the first départe-ment in France to pay its taxes! This elegantly restrained and beautiful square is one of the few true Renaissance structures in Paris. Nine identical brick-fronted houses line each side, broken only by the porti-coed pavilions of the King and Queen (Henry and his wife lived separate lives). Underneath is a colonnade which now shelters small antique shops and restaur-ants. The open square was popular for promenading and duels until the garden was created in 1685. Richelieu lived at no. 21; at no. 6 in the **Hôtel de Rohan-Guéménée** you can visit a museum dedicated to Victor Hugo, who lived here from 1832–48.

Around this stately square sprang up a new district as the rich and titled scrambled for a place in the heart of fashion. The result is a harmonious maze of small streets and squares, complete with some 100 surviving 17th- and 18th-century mansions. Although the area became very run down, it miraculously survived the post-war bulldozers and is today a conservation area of enormous charm and character.

The **Musée Carnavalet**, *23 rue de Sévigné, 3rd*, is housed in the Hôtel Carnavalet, built in 1548, but heavily altered by Mansart in 1655–60. In the courtyard is

> ### HENRI IV
>
> Born in 1553, son of the Duc de Vendôme and the Queen of Navarre, Henri began his political life as commander-in-chief of the Huguenot forces during the Wars of Religion. His marriage to Marguerite de Valois in 1572, sister of Charles IX, meant to symbolise the peace treaty, was in fact used to spark the horrendous St Bartholomew's Day Massacre, organised by his mother-in-law, Cathérine de Medici. In 1593, Henri converted to Catholicism in order to inherit the crown of France, supposedly saying "Paris is worth a mass." His heart always remained Protestant, however, and, in 1598, he signed the Edict of Nantes, guaranteeing free-dom of worship.
>
> He married a second time in 1600, to Marie de Medici. It was an unhappy liaison and though they did manage to produce a son and heir, Louis XIII, they lived separate lives, both indulging in numerous affairs. Henri was assassinated in 1610 by a fanatical Jesuit student. He is still remem-bered fondly as one of the greatest, most liberal and most efficient of French kings.

Left: *An equestrian statue of Louis XIII surveys the elegant and architecturally consistent Place des Vosges laid out by Henri IV.*

Above: *This bakery caters for the Jewish community, which has been established in Paris for 700 years.*

MARAIS WALK

Start at metro St Paul. Go right along Rue St Antoine, past the Church of St Louis-St Paul and the Hôtel de Sully. Turn left up Rue de Birague into Place des Vosges. At the top of the square, turn left into Rue des Francs Bourgeois, right into Rue Sévigné, past the Musée Carnavalet and left into Rue du Parc Royal. To the right, on Rue Thorigny, is the Musée Picasso. Go straight on. The road becomes Rue des 4 Fils. Turn left into Rue des Archives and left again, back onto Rue des Francs Bourgeois. Turn right on Rue Pavée and you will come out on Rue St Antoine, near the metro station.

a magnificent statue of Louis XIV by Coysevox. The museum is dedicated to the history of Paris as told through art. In theory, it runs in chronological order, but it is a total maze and virtually impossible to navigate successfully. Exhibits include several complete rooms, among them the suite of a former owner, 18th-century society hostess and renowned letter writer, Madame de Sévigné; Marcel Proust's cork-lined bedroom; the Art Nouveau Fouquet jewellery boutique; and the 1924 ballroom of the Hôtel Wendel, painted by José-María Sert. Look also for the detailed model of Paris in 1527, a model of the Bastille carved from one of its stones (a popular and lucrative souvenir), a toy guillotine, and the roomful of shop signs. Above all, there are paintings documenting almost every important person and event in the history of the city.

The **Musée Picasso**, *5 rue de Thorigny, 3rd*, is housed in the Hôtel Salé, built in 1656 by Jean Boullier, who made his fortune in salt tax. Inside is a superb collection of work by the late, great Pablo (1881–1973), donated to the state in lieu of inheritance tax. There are few major works, but every period is represented in 200 paintings, 3000 drawings and engravings, and every medium from ceramics to illustrated manuscripts. A sculpture garden, an audio-visual room and a gallery dedicated to Picasso's own collection, with works by Braque, Cézanne, Matisse and Rousseau, completes the exhibition.

Ernest Cognac (1839–1928), wealthy founder of La Samaritaine (*see page 39*) and his wife, Louise Jay, were passionate devotees of 18th-century art. Their private collection forms the core of the delightful **Musée Cognacq-Jay**, *Hôtel Donon, 8 rue Elzévir, 3rd*, dedicated to a period of charming froth. Works by Canaletto, Fragonard and Boucher add weight.

There are several other small museums in the area, all in palatial houses whose architecture alone is worth a look. The **Musée d'Art et d'Histoire du Judaïsme** is situated in the beautiful 17th-century Hôtel de Saint Aignan, *71 rue du Temple, 3rd, (metro Rambuteau),* tel: 01 53 01 86 60, web: www.mahj.org The museum traces the evolution of Jewish communities from the Middle Ages to the present, focusing on the Jews in France. It was formed by combining Jewish art, crafts and ritual objects from Eastern Europe and North Africa of the Musée d'Art Juif with medieval Jewish artefacts from the Musée National du Moyen Age. Highlights include documents relating to the Dreyfus Affair and works by Chagall, Modigliani and Soutine. The museum is open from 11:00–18:00 Mon–Fri and 10:00–18:00 Sun.

The **Musée des Arts et Métiers**, in the former priory of St-Nicholas-des-Champs, *60 rue de Réaumur, 3rd (metro: Arts et Métiers, Strasbourg St Denis)*, traces the development of science and technology from the 18th to the 20th century. The documentary **Musée de l'Histoire de France** offers the only public access to the National Archives and two of the most magnificent buildings in the Marais, the Hôtel de Soubise (1554 and rebuilt in 1705), *60 rue des Francs-Bourgeois, 4th*, and the Hôtel de Rohan (1705), *87 rue Vieille du Temple, 4th*. Open 13:45–17:45, closed Tue. The **Musée de la Chasse et de Nature**, Hôtel Guénégaud (*c*1650), *60 rue des Archives, 3rd*, has dead animals and paintings of hunting. The **Musée de la Serrure**, Hôtel Libéral Bruant (1685), *1 rue de la Perle, 3rd*, has a collection of locks, from the Roman era onwards. The **Bibliothèque Historique de la Ville de Paris** is in the Hôtel Lamoignan (1518 and 1612), *24 rue Pavée, 4th*. The **Pavillon de l'Arsénal** (1564), *21 boulevard Morland, 4th*, has an exhibition about the history, and future architectural planning, of Paris.

Finally, take a look at two other houses, the brick-patterned **Maison de Jacques Coeur** (*c*1440), *rue des Archives, 4th*, built by Charles VII's financial adviser,

---

DEATHLY PROTEST

In 1627, Cardinal Richelieu banned duelling. On 12 May, a group of six hot-headed noblemen gathered in front of his windows at 21 Place des Vosges, to fight a duel in protest. The Comte de Montmorency, La Berthe and des Chapelles took on the Marquise de Beuvron, Bussy d'Amboise and Buquet. Bussy was killed, La Berthe was wounded and Beuvron and Buquet escaped to England. Montmorency and des Chapelles were not so lucky. Arrested and condemned to death, they were beheaded in the Grève (now place de l'Hôtel de Ville).

and one of the oldest houses in Paris. Framed for poisoning the king's mistress, Coeur was stripped of all lands and money. His innocence was acknowledged a year after his death in exile in 1457. The **Hôtel de Beauvais** (1657), *68 rue François-Miron, 4th*, was built by Catherine Belliers, a maid ennobled by Marie de Medici for her ability to give a good enema and for assuring the queen, from first-hand experience, of her son's sexual prowess! Other particularly fine houses include: **Hôtel des Ambassadeurs de Hollande** (1655; also known as Amelot de Bisseuil), *47 rue Vieille du Temple, 3rd*; **Hôtel d'Aumont** (1645), *7 rue de Jouy, 4th*; **Maison de Jean Hérouët** (1510), *42 rue des Francs-Bourgeois, 4th*; and **Hôtel de Sens** (1475-1507), *1 rue du Figuier, 4th*.

Since the 13th century the Marais has also been home to the Jewish community in Paris, centred on the **Rue des Rosiers**. A new wave of settlement by Sephardic Jews from North Africa revived the area after World War II and you will find several working synagogues and Jewish restaurants in the area. The **Mémorial du Martyr Juif Inconnu**, *17 rue Geoffroy l'Asnier, 4th*, has a small museum about the Jewish struggle against Nazism and an eternal flame for victims of the Holocaust.

Rue St Antoine, the widest street in the district, is an extension of the Rue de Rivoli, based on a Roman road. In 1559 Montgomery, the Scottish captain of the guards, fatally wounded Henry II during a tournament here to celebrate the marriage

Below: *The archway to the Hôtel de Sully. The façade of the building has been restored to its original 17th-century appearance.*

ST GERVAIS-ST PROTAIS

At the corner of the Rue François-Miron, following the route of the old Roman road from Paris to Senlis, is the church of St Gervais and St Protais. Dedicated to two Roman martyrs, the church was founded in the 6th century, but the present building dates from the 16th. Its façade displays all three orders of classical architecture – Doric, Ionic and Corinthian – while the interior is Gothic with interesting decorative details. The church is most known for its connections with music, and several members of the Couperin family were employed there as organists over a period of 170 years, among them composer François Couperin (1668–1733). Place St Gervais is also noteworthy for its elm tree, under which judicicial decisions were made in the Middle Ages.

of Henry's daughter to Phillip II of Spain. Montgomery fled, and the king died ten days later in the Hôtel de Tournelles. His widow, Cathérine de Medici, tore down the building and, 15 years later, captured and executed Montgomery, as soon as he set foot on French soil. The **Eglise de St-Louis-St-Paul** was built by the Jesuits in 1641. Once equally luxuriant inside and out, it lost its fine furnishings during the Revolution and seems spartan these days. The beautiful **Hôtel de Sully** (1625), no. 62, now houses the Centre des Monuments Nationaux, and has a superb bookshop that specializes in all things Parisian.

LETTRES DE CACHET

One of the most notorious aspects of the Bastille was the *lettre de cachet*. The kings regularly signed piles of these blank arrest warrants. Anyone with a grudge who could get hold of one simply filled in the name and his enemy would be held indefinitely and without trial in the Bastille. The system was abolished in 1784 but among those who had already fallen victim were Voltaire, the Marquis de Sade and the enigmatic and unnamed Man in the Iron Mask.

BASTILLE

Not a trace remains of the Bastille, except an outline in the paving stones of the **Place de la Bastille** *(metro: Bastille)* and a short stretch of the foundations, seen from the metro platform (Line 5). Built in 1367–82 to guard the eastern Porte St Antoine against the British, the fortress expanded into a huge castle with eight towers. In spite of this, it was captured six times in seven sieges. As a prison, it was used mainly to lock up those who offended the king and nothing like as grim as the Conciergerie and Châtelet. Many of the wealthy inmates had comfortably furnished rooms, good meals and their own servants. Ironically, the government gave the order to demolish the prison two weeks before the crowd did it for them on 14 July 1789, a date which is celebrated annually by the French. When the 600-strong mob arrived, they found only seven prisoners left to free – and only one of them was a political detainee. Citizen Palloy, who took charge of the demolition, made a fortune selling the stones for building or carving them into models of the Bastille as souvenirs.

Napoleon's plans to erect a 6m (20ft) bronze elephant in the newly formed square came to nothing and its plinth was used to erect the **Colonne de Juillet 1830**, as a memorial to those who died in the three-day 1830 revolution.

The cool, crisp **Opéra Bastille**, designed by Carlos Ott, a Canadian-Uruguayan architect, was opened in 1989 to celebrate the Bicentennial of the Revolution and has helped to resurrect a run-down area. The existing Opéra was renamed Opéra Garnier (*see* page 67) to avoid confusion. Also redeveloped are the former arcades of a railway bridge. The popular **Viaduc des Arts** *(metro: Bastille)* along Avenue Daumesnil has brought a wealth of craftsmen and artisans to the often neglected 12th arrondissement.

Opposite: *The infamous Bastille prison is now only a tracing in the pavement. In its place stand the 1830 July Column and the Paris Opéra, built in 1989.*

The Cimetière du Père Lachaise ✶✶
(metro: Père Lachaise, Philippe-Auguste)
Named after Louis XIV's confessor and established in 1804, this has become the largest and most interesting of the great Parisian cemeteries, with a starry list of inhabitants,

many of whom were moved from elsewhere to help popularize it. Many of its tombs are impressive monuments and the cemetery is visited as much for its sculptural contents as for its occupants. A map of celebrity graves is available at the gate. Writers include Fontaine, Molière, Beaumarchais, Colette, Proust, Balzac, Hugo, Oscar Wilde and Gertrude Stein. Musicians include Chopin, Fauré, Rossini, Bizet, Edith Piaf, Jim Morrison (of The Doors). Art lovers should look for Corot, Bellini, David, Modigliani and Delacroix, and theatregoers for Sarah Bernhardt, Simone Signoret and Isadora Duncan. Other notables include Baron Haussmann, Marshal Ney and Abélard and Héloïse.

The Paris Commune made its last stand here on 27 May 1871. Many died during the fighting and the last 147 alive were shot against the Mur des Fédérés, in the southeast corner. They are buried where they fell, in a communal grave where flowers are still left.

There is also a memorial to the many French who died in Nazi concentration camps or as a result of their work with the French Resistance during World War II.

ABELARD AND HELOISE

Brilliant 12th-century philosopher, Peter Abélard (1079–1142) fell passionately in love with his pupil, Héloïse, the beautiful niece of his landlord, Canon Filbert. Héloïse (1101–1164) refused to marry him, and when she became pregnant, Abélard packed her off to a convent, where she lived to a ripe old age and became abbess. Her enraged uncle had Abélard castrated. He retaliated; the canon lost his home, position and wealth. Abélard then retired to a monastery in St Denis. Although the couple corresponded, they never met again while alive, but are buried together in Père Lachaise Cemetery.

4
Montmartre and
the Northeast

MONTMARTRE ★★★

(metro: Anvers – for the funicular, Abbesses, Lamarck-Caulaincourt)

A centre of prehistoric sun worship, dedicated to Mercury by the Romans, 129m (423 ft) high Montmartre was renamed in the 9th century after St Denis, martyred here in AD262 (*see* page 99). It is the highest point in Paris, known to locals simply as 'la butte' (the hill). There is an excellent view from the steps of the basilica.

Until Haussmann enclosed it within the city walls in 1860, Montmartre remained a small, relatively peaceful village. Henry IV brought canons up here during his siege, and Cossacks occupied the area after Napoleon's downfall in 1814. In 1871, however, the National Guard holed up here and declared the Paris Commune (*see* page 14), an action which led to 20,000 deaths and the near destruction of Paris.

Meanwhile, in 1673–89, a local nun had several visions of Christ, who asked for a church of the Sacred Heart. During the dark days of the Franco-Prussian War (1870–71), two businessmen vowed to build it if France were spared; the church was eventually completed in 1910 and consecrated in 1919. The huge sugary-white dome of the **Basilique du Sacré Cœur** now dominates the skyline of Paris. The fanciful architect, Paul Abadie, who delighted in sticking Byzantine domes on everything he built, let his imagination run riot, creating a magnificent pastiche that has most architectural critics foaming at the mouth, but is adored by those who appreciate late Victorian architecture.

MONTMARTRE WALK

Start at the top of the funicular. Visit the Basilica, then walk down past St Pierre, turn left, then right into Rue du Mont Cenis. Take the first left, then right into Rue des Saules. Turn left and walk to the Place du Tertre. From here, head downhill on Rue Lépic. Near the bottom, it becomes Rue des Abbesses, leading into Place des Abbesses, where you will find a metro stop.

Opposite: *The glistening basilica of Sacré Cœur was built by the nation as a mark of repentance and devotion after the Franco-Prussian War.*

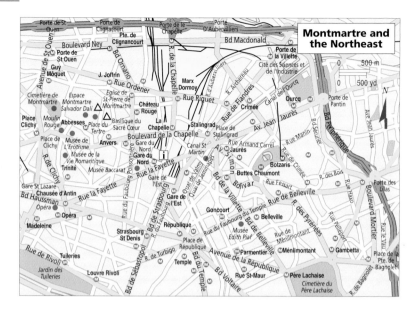

Montmartre and the Northeast

0   500 m

0   500 yd

N

Inside, Luc Olivier Merson's vast mosaic of Christ
swoops over the high altar, arms akimbo, the heroes of
France at his feet. Since 1 August 1885, without exception, a rota of conservative locals have prayed here every
hour for the sins of the Commune to be forgiven.

Founded by Louis VI and Queen Adelaide of Savoy
(who later became the first abbess) in 1133 as part of a
once-powerful convent, the **Eglise de St-Pierre de
Montmartre**, *place St Pierre, 18th*, is totally dwarfed. It
has some fine Romanesque capitals, an 18th-century
façade, and 20th-century stained glass.

But to most people, Montmartre is all about its glory
years as the focus of the artistic world. The artists began
to arrive in about 1840, drawn in by the paintable surroundings, golden light and cheap rents. They lived
mainly on the breadline – Puccini based his tragic opera
La Bohème on their uncomfortable existence – yet they
tapped a well of genius and created a legend that draws
millions to Paris each year. By about 1920 rents had risen
and the artists moved to Montparnasse.

The focus of the 'village', the pretty **Place du Tertre**, is now a heaving mass of pavement artists (licensed at two easels per square metre) and gawping tourists. It is still fun to look and the atmosphere bubbles, but most of the art is sadly third-rate while the many cafés and restaurants are grossly overpriced. **La Mère Cathérine**, *6 rue Norvins, 18th,* founded in 1793, is said to have been where the term 'bistro' originated, coined by Cossack forces in search of quick service (*see* page 28). Nearby, the cavernous **Espace Montmartre Salvador Dali**, *11 rue Poulbot, 18th,* has a beautifully displayed collection of over 300 paintings, drawings and sculptures by the master surrealist.

Several of the greatest local artists, including Renoir, Van Gogh, Dufy, Suzanne Valadon and Utrillo, all lived at *12–14 rue Cortot, 18th.* Today, it is home to the **Musée de Montmartre**, dedicated to the history and artistic life of the hill, with old photos, maps and plans, posters by Toulouse-Lautrec and other Bohemian memorabilia.

Beyond this, the deceptively rustic **Lapin Agile**, *22 rue des Saules, 18th,* is a famous cabaret, home to some

Above: *The brightly canopied cafés of the Place du Tertre just round the corner from the Sacré Cœur provide an ideal setting for artists keen to sell souvenir paintings of Montmartre.*

DON'T MISS

*** **Sacré Cœur**: overblown and fantastic, this church is a glorious folly, with superb views.
*** **The streets and cafés of Montmartre.**
*** **The Cité des Sciences**: Paris' homage to science and technology.

of the most biting satirical comedy in Paris. It gained its name from the delightful sign of a rabbit escaping from a cooking pot, painted by André Gill (le lapin à Gill). A little further on, the last **vineyard** in Paris was replanted in 1886. The grapes are harvested amidst great festivities on the first Saturday in October each year and crushed for a very indifferent gamay, *Clos de Montmartre*, sold in aid of the local old people.

Rue Lepic is the longest and most gentle route up the hill. At no. 77, the much-painted **Moulin de la Gallette** (1622), is one of two surviving windmills (out of an original 30). In 1814 the Cossacks crucified the miller on one of the sails, after which the family decided to give up on flour. Further down the road, there is a good market.

Pigalle is best known for its nightlife, centred on the famous **Moulin Rouge**, *82 boulevard de Clichy, 18th*, which opened in 1889 and is still going strong. The side streets support a bevy of prostitutes and clubs to cater for all tastes. Single women should avoid the area after dark. The turquoise tile and brick-clad church of **St Jean l'Evangéliste**, *Place des Abbesses, 18th*, was designed by Anatole de Baudot (1904), the first church in France to be built in concrete. The **Chapelle du Martyre**, *9 rue Yvonne-le-Tac, 18th*, is the latest 19th-century chapel on the spot where St Denis was martyred. In 1534 St Ignatius Loyola and his followers

Left: *The Moulin Rouge has been famous for its Parisian nightlife since the 1890s and was painted by the artist Toulouse-Lautrec.*
Opposite, top: *Painted café sign.*
Opposite, bottom: *The quaint charm of Le Lapin Agile belies its reputation as a hotbed of satire.*

gathered in the crypt to found the Society of Jesus (the Jesuits). The delightful **Musée d'Art Naïf Max Fournay**, Halle-St-Pierre, *2 rue Ronsard, 18th*, has a cheerful, unusual collection of naive art and children's exhibitions and workshops.

The **Cimetière de Montmartre**, *20 av Rachel, 18th (metro: place de Clichy)*, is a romantic Parisian cemetery founded in the 19th century. Inhabitants include Stendhal, Zola, Fragonard, Berlioz, Degas, Nijinsky, Delibes, Offenbach, François Truffaut and Alphonsine Plessis.

Other museums in the area include **Musée Edith Piaf**, *5 rue Crespin-du-Gast, 11th (metro: Ménilmontant)*. A superb singer, the 'little sparrow' (1915–63) was born on a street corner but went on to become the toast of the world (*see page 58*). Open by appointment; tel: 01 43 55 52 72. The **Musée de L'Érotisme**, *72 bd de Clichy, 18th (metro: Blanche)*, offers an extraordinary range of exhibits and is open 16 hours a day. The **Musée de la Vie Romantique**, *16 rue Chaptal, 9th (metro: St Georges, Blanche)*, has memoirs of George Sand, and her family and inner circle in a typically bourgeois 19th-century home. The **Musée Baccarat**, *30bis rue Paradis, 10th (metro: Gare de l'Est)*, is the glittering showpiece of the crystal factory founded in 1764.

In 1860 Haussmann turned a deserted quarry and rubbish dump into the delightful **Parc des Buttes-Chaumont**, *rue Manin, 19th (metro: Botzaris, Buttes-Chaumont)*, with tumbling water, cliffs and lavish greenery.

STREET ARCHITECTURE

The Place des Abbesses is a good monument to two of the least known artistic patrons of Paris. The splendid, swirling metro entrance is a rare surviving example of the original design by Art Nouveau architect, Hector Guimard (1867–1942). The small, green drinking fountain is one of many donated to Paris by the 19th-century English philanthropist, Sir Richard Wallace (1818–90), who also ran two field hospitals and several feeding stations during the 1870–71 siege. His private art collection is now on display in London.

Above: *The Bassin de la Villette is a dock for the Parisian network of canals, and is in turn linked to the Seine by the Canal St Martin.*

Parc de la Villette ★★★

30 av. Corentin-Cariou, 19th (metro: Porte de la Villette)
For over a century this seedy quarter was home to the Paris stockyards, a chaos of live animals, abattoirs and butchers. In the 1960s refrigeration came in and the whole web collapsed, leaving the world's largest slaughter-house empty. In 1993 a 55ha (136 acre) showcase complex rose like a phoenix, with the aid of architect Adrian Fainsilber, to become one of the top attractions in Paris.

To get there the most enjoyable way, take a boat trip along the pretty **Canal St Martin**, which connects the Seine with the **Bassin de la Villette** (1806), and beyond that, the Canal de l'Ourcq (*see* page 120). It was built in 1825 for handling freight; for 2km (1¹/₄ miles) it runs underground. The charming round **Rotonde de la Villette** (1784) was built as a customs house.

The slaughterhouse itself has become the super high-tech **Cité des Sciences et de l'Industrie**, a sparkling inter-active hands-on museum designed to keep all ages and people, including the most technically inept, enthralled for hours. The main body is known as the **Explora**, with two vast floors dedicated to permanent exhibitions on Space, the Ocean, the Environment, Cultivating Land, Bio-technology, Language and Communication, Mathematics, Sound, Light, Energy, Health and the Human Body, Computer Technology, the Earth, Sea and Stars. A high-tech soil-free greenhouse and a supersonic bomber are suspended in the rafters and there is a special Cité des Enfants for 3–12 year olds, with plenty for them to do.

Inside the Explora on the second floor is a **Planetarium**. Outside, the **Géode** is a massive geodesic sphere made of 6500 stainless steel triangles, with a 1000m² (10,750 sq ft) hemispherical cinema screen. The

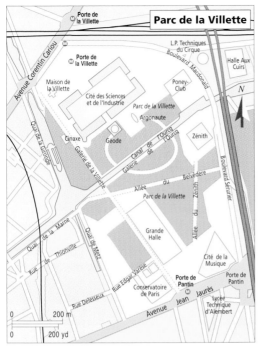

even more unsettling **Cinaxe** moves and shakes the entire cinema as you watch. The **Cité de la Musique** has music and dance schools, workshop and performance spaces and the **Musée de la Musique**. There is also a theatre, and the Grande Halle is used for concerts.

Other attractions include the park itself, with playgrounds and sculptures, follies, and even an example of a 1957 submarine, **Argonaute**. The **Zénith** is a huge polyester tent that holds 6000, designed as a concert venue.

Below: *The gigantic Géode screen at the Cité des Sciences et de l'Industrie invites the visitor to glimpse a futuristic world.*

5
The Louvre and Opéra

THE LOUVRE ★★★

(metro: Louvre-Rivoli, Palais-Royal)

The Louvre is not only one of the greatest art galleries, but also the largest royal palace in the world. Allow plenty of time, wear comfortable shoes and don't even try to see everything. It is a sightseeing marathon with 32km (18 miles) of corridors.

The first fortress was built here by Philippe-Auguste in 1204–23; since then numerous monarchs have extended the vast, lavish patchwork of palatial apartments and courtyards. Around the central Cour Napoléon are the northern Richelieu Wing, the southern section of the palace, the Denon Wing, and the eastern Sully Wing which leads through to the Cour Carrée and Claude Perrault's 17th-century colonnade. An excavated area shows the remnants of the early fortress. To the right are the Jardin du Carrousel and Jardin des Tuileries.

The ultra-modern glass pyramid was added in 1991 by architect I. M. Pei, as the new main entrance to the museum. From the Halle Napoléon separate escalators lead to the three wings. A free colour-coded plan is available to help you find your personal highlights. Blue is for ground floor; red for first floor; and yellow, second floor. The prize exhibits are always surrounded by vast crowds; elsewhere there are equally stunning works of art with half the number of people.

Most famous of all is the *Mona Lisa* (*La Joconde* in French), in the Denon Wing, brought to the city by Leonardo da Vinci himself, during the reign of François I,

LE GRANDE AXE HISTORIQUE

This triumphant way sweeping through the heart of Paris was laid out by the 17th-century landscape gardener, Le Nôtre. It starts in the courtyard of the Louvre with the Arc du Carrousel (25m [82ft]), runs across the Place de la Concorde and up the Champs-Elysées to the Arc de Triomphe (50m [164ft]) and culminates in the Grande Arche de la Défense (100m [328ft]). The length is about 8km (5 miles); both the courtyard of the Louvre and the Grand Arche are angled at 6° 33' from the line of the Axe.

Opposite: *I. M. Pei's glass pyramid is a controversial contribution to the Louvre.*

The Louvre

1 Arc de Triomphe du Carrousel
2 Cour Lefuel
3 Pavillon Denon
4 Cour Visconti
5 Cour du Sphinx
6 Pavillon des Arts
7 Pavillon du Petit Bourbon
8 Pavillon de L'Oratoire
9 Pavillon Sully
10 Cour de la Poste
11 Pavillon Colbert
12 Cour des Caisses
13 Pavillon Richelieu
14 Cour du Ministre
15 Porte Denon
16 Comédie Française
17 Musée de la Mode et du Textile, Musée de la Publicité and Musée des Arts Décoratifs

Below: *Model boats for hire to sail on the Octagonal Basin in the Jardin des Tuileries.*

who started the collection with twelve paintings by the masters of the day. His royal successors were also avid collectors and by the time the museum opened in 1793 it was already one of the richest bodies of art in the world. Almost every great European artist is represented here. Amongst the paintings, look out for the satirical *Ship of Fools* (Hieronymus Bosch); Leonardo's exquisite *Virgin with the Infant Jesus and St Anne* and *Virgin of the Rocks*; Botticelli's *Venus and the Graces*; and Vermeer's *Lacemaker*. The finer sculptures include the *Marly Horses* (Guillaume Costou) which originally graced the Place de la Concorde, and Michelangelo's *Slaves*.

The 2nd-century BC *Venus de Milo*, bought from the Greeks in 1820, is the highlight of the vast Ancient collection, which covers the Roman, Greek, Etruscan, Egyptian and several Middle Eastern civilizations. Other highlights include the vast granite *Sphinx* and *Squatting Scribe* (both 4th dynasty, *c*2500BC), and the Greek *Winged Victory of Samothrace*.

Left: The Pope Being Shown Building Plans *on view in the Louvre.*

The biggest draw amongst the objets d'art is usually the magnificent 140-carat *Regent Diamond* which can be seen amongst the Crown Jewels.

Also in the palace at *107 rue de Rivoli, 1st,* are the **Musée de la Mode et du Textile**, dedicated to the history of fashion with a gorgeous collection of haute couture and historical costumes; the **Musée de la Publicité**, dedicated to the 19th-century advertising industry; and the **Musée des Arts Décoratifs**, dedicated to decorative and ornamental art, furniture and furnishings from the Middle Ages to the present day. Look out for the Art Nouveau and Art Deco rooms, the collection of 60,000 posters and the dolls *(metro: Palais-Royal, Tuileries).*

The **Arc de Triomphe du Carrousel**, built by Napoleon to mark his 1805 victories, is closely modelled on the Roman Arch of Septimius Severus. It was originally topped by the four famous horses of St Mark's, Venice; they were returned in 1815 along with all the other artistic treasures Napoleon had looted from around Europe. Beyond this stretch the **Jardin des Tuileries**. In 1560 Cathérine de Medici bought a derelict tile works *(tuileries)* and laid out the first gardens. They were redesigned by Le Nôtre in 1664 and still follow his formal plan, with small lawns, serried rows of identical

---

TIMETABLE OF THE LOUVRE

1204–23 Philippe-Auguste builds first fortress.
1360s Charles V converts it to a royal residence.
1527–46 François I starts to convert it into a Renaissance palace. Work, overseen by Lescot, continues through the reigns of Henry II, Charles IX and Henry III.
1563 Cathérine de Medici commissions Philippe Delorme to build the Palais des Tuileries and Waterside Gallery. Work continues until Henry IV's death in 1610.
1627 Louis XIII builds the Pavillon de l'Horloge.
1659–70 Louis XIV builds the Cour Carrée and extends the Tuileries.
1678 Louis XIV moves court to Versailles
1793 Museum opens.
1805–15 Napoleon extends the northern arm to the Pavillon de Marsan.
1852–70 Napoleon III builds new pavilions around the Cour Napoléon.
1988–9 I. M. Pei adds the glass pyramid.

plants and wide walkways lined by uncomfortable
benches. There are several fine statues, including four by
Rodin, but the one real point of gaiety is the Octagonal
Basin, a large pond surrounded by a phalanx of ice-
cream sellers, where generations of children have sailed
their colourful toy boats.

At the far end is the enchanting **Musée de l'Orangerie**,
place de la Concorde, 1st (metro: Concorde), home to an excellent small collection, including works by Cézanne,
Matisse, Renoir, Utrillo, Sisley and Soutine. At its heart is a
place of almost magical serenity designed to house, in perfect surroundings, eight of Monet's vast, almost abstract

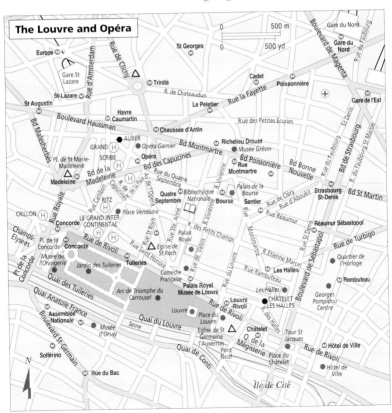

Left: The Palais Royal was rebuilt in the 18th century by Duke Philippe II, but it was his grandson Louis-Philippe who enclosed the gardens on three sides with arcades of shops in order to provide an income.

waterlily paintings. The museum is closed for renovation but due to reopen in January 2006; web: www.rmn.fr Next door, the **Jeu de Paume**, *20 rue Royale, 1st (metro: Concorde, Tuileries)*, is a former 'real tennis' court which hosts regular temporary exhibitions of modern art.

The **Palais Royal** *(metro: Palais Royal)* was built in 1624 for Cardinal Richelieu. He left it to Louis XIV (in case he was short of palaces), who handed it on to his brother, Philippe d'Orléans. The palace is closed to the public, but the delightful colonnaded galleries and gardens are accessible. In 1781 Philippe sold off building lots around the gardens, creating an enclosed, popular centre of drinking, gambling and prostitution (now all gone). The steel balls in the fountains and the black and white pillars in the court were added in 1986 by Daniel Buren.

To one side of the main entrance, the 1786 **Comédie Française**, *2 rue de Richelieu, 1st*, is still home to the country's most prestigious theatre company (*see page 21*). In the foyer is the chair in which Molière died in 1673, on stage during a performance of *Le Malade Imaginaire*. Behind the palace is the **Bibliothèque Nationale**, *52 rue de Richelieu, 1st (metro: Bourse)*. Over 12 million publications, some dating back an extraordinary six centuries, were formerly housed in this building. However, as the collection increased, new premises were required and, under President Mitterrand, a new **Bibliothèque Nationale de France** was constructed in the 13th where

WALK

Start at metro Palais-Royal and walk west along Rue de Rivoli. Turn right into Rue Castiglione, cross Place Vendôme and continue up Rue de la Paix to the Place de l'Opéra. Turn left along Boulevard des Capucines, which turns into Boulevard de la Madeleine, coming out beside the Eglise de la Madeleine (*see page 71*). Walk down into Place de la Concorde, turn into the Tuileries Gardens and follow them back to the Louvre courtyard, and from there back to the metro.

Above: *The Jardin des Tuileries provide a tranquil haven in the midst of a bustling city.*

this priceless collection is now found. But this Bibliothèque is still worth a visit for its glorious little museum, the **Cabinet des Médailles et des Antiques**, containing the treasure-trove of the kings of France, St-Denis and the Sainte-Chapelle. Lovers of expensive baubles and things that gleam will be in their element. Nearby are also several charming arcades, including the Galerie Véro-Dodat, Galerie Colbert and Galerie Vivienne.

The **Eglise de St Roch** (patron saint of plague victims), *rue St-Honoré, 1st (metro: Tuileries)*, was built in 1653–1730. Regular outbreaks of plague stopped at about the same time. The bullet holes in the façade were added on 5 October 1795, when Napoleon led an artillery troop against a royalist uprising. As a reward, he was given command of the French troops in Italy. Inside are several fine paintings and the tombs of Le Nôtre and Corneille.

As well as all his other building work, Louis XIV felt he needed to add two new royal squares to Paris. The larger **Place Vendôme**, built in 1687–1721 by Hardouin-Mansart, is a gracious Classical octagon surrounded by an arcade and named after the Hôtel Vendôme which had previously occupied the site. Napoleon erected the **Vendôme Column** to commemorate his victory at Austerlitz in 1805. A replica of Trajan's Column in Rome, it stands 44m (144ft) high, has a stone core around which is a spiral of bronze reliefs, cast from 1250 cannons captured during the battle. The whole column is a copy of the original, destroyed in 1871. The harmony of the **Place des Victoires**, a little further east, has been damaged by the ravages of time and revolution. Just north of this, the neoclassical **Bourse**, *place de la Bourse, 2nd (metro: Bourse)*, was designed by Alexandre-Théodore Brongniart. It has been the home of the Paris Stock Exchange since 1808.

OPÉRA

In 1660–1705 Louis XIV knocked down the city wall, filled in the moat and created the Boulevard. From about 1750 the road became a fashionable promenade. In 1860 Haussmann got to work, carving out a series of **Grands Boulevards** – Capucines, Italiens, Madeleine, Montmartre,

Poissonnière, Bonne Nouvelle, Saint-Denis, Saint-Martin. Together, they now make up a heaving shopping centre, the Parisian equivalent of Oxford Street. Pride of place goes to two department stores, Galeries Lafayette and Le Printemps. Galeries Lafayette *(metro: Havre-Caumartin)*, in particular, has beautiful Art Nouveau décor. Nearby, the **Musée Grévin**, *10 boulevard Montmartre, 9th (metro: Montmartre)*, is a waxworks museum inspired by Madame Tussaud's and beloved by children.

At the crossroads of six boulevards, in the Place de l'Opéra *(metro: Opéra)* sits Napoleon III's magnificently pompous **Opéra Garnier** (after the architect, Charles Garnier), which opened in 1875. The design is a hotchpotch of grandiose styles, covered in relief busts of famous musicians, Classical columns and baroque statuary. Inside, Garnier used multi-coloured marble from every quarry in France, more statues and lashings of gold leaf. The unexpected highlight, however, is painter Marc Chagall's glorious, swirling ceiling under the dome, painted in 1964. Astonishingly, the largest theatre in the world can only seat 2200 people. The rest is taken up by a vast stage and endless galleries and basements of dressing rooms, wardrobes, and workshops which provided the subterranean inspiration for Gaston Leroux's *Fantôme de l' Opéra*, about the horribly deformed phantom who lurks beneath the theatre and falls in love with a young singer. There is a small museum and library here and you can do guided tours (tel: 08 92 89 90 90; web: www.opera-de-paris.fr

Below: *The magnificent central glass dome of Galeries Lafayette adds a special sense of occasion to shopping.*

6
Northwest Paris: the Rive Droite

Place de la Concorde ★★

This cavernous square *(metro: Concorde)*, laid out in 1755–75 by Jacques-Ange Gabriel for Louis XV, was designed as a promenade – hard to imagine as you dodge the swirling, lethal traffic. It is built up only on one side, with two supremely elegant colonnaded buildings; the Hôtel de la Marine (right), and one of Paris' most luxurious hotels, the Hôtel Crillon (left). To the east are the Tuileries (*see* page 63); to the south, the river. To the west, copies of Coustou's superb 18th-century Marly horses mark the entrance to the Champs-Elysées (the originals are in the Louvre for safe-keeping).

The huge central octagon has a statue at each point representing great cities of France (clockwise from the bridge: Bordeaux, Nantes, Brest, Rouen, Lille, Strasbourg, Lyons, and Marseilles). Within it are two huge, ornate 19th-century bronze fountains, dripping with bearded gods, mermaids and fish, by Jacques Hittorff, and the 75m (250ft) pink granite **obelisk**, carved in Luxor *c*1250BC and given to France by Muhammed Ali, the Ottoman governor of Egypt, in 1831. The **Pont de la Concorde** was completed in 1791 using stones from the newly demolished Bastille.

In 1770, during the wedding celebrations of the Dauphin and Marie-Antoinette, a stand collapsed killing 133 people. During much of the Revolution, the Place became home to the guillotine. Both Louis XVI and Marie-Antoinette were beheaded here near the Brest statue. It was given its eventual name of Concorde as a gesture of reconciliation.

PARIS
Rive Droite

Seine

Boulevard Périphérique

WALK

Start in the Place de la Concorde. Turn right, cross the Cours la Reine and down onto the quay. Walk past the houseboats to Pont Alexandre III. Climb up, take Av. Churchill, between the Grand and Petit Palais and turn left onto the Champs-Elysées. At Rond Point, turn left onto Av. Montaigne and follow this to Place de l'Alma (with metro and Bâteau Mouche stops). Alternatively, take Av. George V back up to the Champs-Elysées and turn left for the Arc de Triomphe, or right for the Place de la Concorde.

Opposite: *The huge Place de la Concorde has magnificent statuary and fountains.*

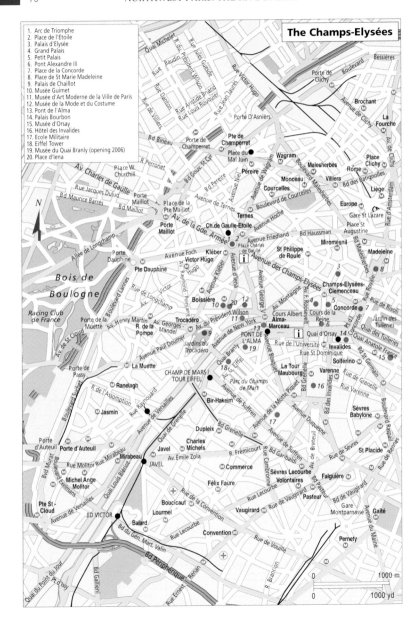

The Champs-Elysées

1. Arc de Triomphe
2. Place de l'Étoile
3. Palais d'Elysée
4. Grand Palais
5. Petit Palais
6. Pont Alexandre III
7. Place de la Concorde
8. Place de St Marie Madeleine
9. Palais de Chaillot
10. Musée Guimet
11. Musée d'Art Moderne de la Ville de Paris
12. Musée de la Mode et du Costume
13. Pont de l'Alma
14. Palais Bourbon
15. Musée d'Orsay
16. Hôtel des Invalides
17. Ecole Militaire
18. Eiffel Tower
19. Musée du Quai Branly (opening 2006)
20. Place d'Iena

Rue Royale, leading north, is one of the richest and most exclusive shopping streets in Paris, a joy for people-watchers and window-shoppers. At the far end, in the Place de Ste Marie Madeleine *(metro: Madeleine)*, the **Eglise de La Madeleine** has confused history and architecture. Work started on the church in 1764 and again in 1777. The half-built site mouldered throughout the Revolution, until, in 1806, Napoleon commissioned Vignon to build the existing Greek temple as a Temple of Glory. In 1815 the Bourbons decided to turn it back into a church. The starkly classical exterior, surrounded by 52 Corinthian columns and a carved frieze, contrasts sharply with the ornately decorated Baroque opulence of the interior.

The Champs-Elysées

In 1667 Louis XIV and André Le Nôtre laid out a promenade, straight on from the Tuileries, through fields of sheep and cows. Extended several times over the next century, a drive through these 'Elysian Fields' gradually came to be a popular outing. The real transformation began when Napoleon chose the hilltop for a triumphal arch, the Arc de Triomphe.

Today the Champs-Elysées is heavily built up with offices and shops, overpriced cinemas, clubs and cafés and few feel inspired to linger. Only the first short section, from Concorde to the Rond Point, remains at all Elysian, flanked by mature trees and parkland.

Just to the right, on av Marigny, the **Palais d'Elysée** is the official home of the President of France. To the left, the truly vast **Grand Palais**, av du Général Eisenhower, and not quite so vast

Below: *No longer a rural promenade, the Champs-Elysées is now a bustling thoroughfare.*

MINOR ART MUSEUMS

Atelier-Musée Henri Bouchard, 25 rue de l'Yvette, 16th (metro: Jasmin). The studio museum of sculptor Henri Bouchard (1875-1960).
Musée Bourdelle, 18 rue Antoine Bordelle, 15th (metro: Falguiére). The house and workshop of Antoine Bordelle (1861–1929) contains monumental bronze sculptures.
Musée Dapper, 35bis rue Paul Valéry, 16th (metro: Victor Hugo) Regular exhibitions of the finest African art.
Musée National Jean-Jaques Henner, 43 av de Villers, 17th (metro: Monceau). Over 700 paintings and drawings by Henner (1829–1905).
Musée Gustave Moreau, 14 rue de la Rochefoucauld, 9th (metro: Trinité). Symbolist painter Moreau (1825–98) lived and worked in this studio, now filled with thousands of his works.

Petit Palais, av Winston Churchill *(metro: Champs Elysées-Clemenceau)* caused a sensation with their innovative use of glass and iron during the Universal Exhibition of 1900. The Petit Palais usually houses the **Musée des Beaux-Arts de la Ville de Paris**, full of sumptuous medieval, Renaissance and 18th-century furniture and *objets d'art* and an inspiring collection of 19th-century French paintings (closed for renovations until the end of 2005). The Grand Palais houses a conference centre, part of the University of Paris, and regular touring exhibitions. To the rear, the **Palais de la Découverte**, av. Franklin D Roosevelt, was transformed for the 1937 Exhibition. Until the opening of the Cité des Sciences *(see page 58)*, this was the premier science museum in Paris. It now seems a little faded, but is still fascinating with plenty of entertaining hands-on experiments.

The spectacular **Pont Alexandre III**, named after the Czar of Russia who laid the foundation stone in 1896, was also built for the 1900 Exhibition. Dedicated to a new alliance between Russia and France, it bears the coats of arms of the two countries. It is the most beautiful of all the Paris bridges, a joyous affirmation of the Belle Epoque, flamboyant with gilded cherubs, winged horses, lions, garlands of flowers, birds, shells and shields.

Avenue Montaigne is the global heart of haute couture, home to many of the world's greatest designers *(see page 121)*. Most also have other outlets handling the real money-makers of prêt-à-porter (ready-to-wear), perfume and make-up. Couturier fashion is little more than a glamorous loss-leader these days.

The top of the hill is crowned by one of the city's most familiar icons. In 1806 Napoleon commissioned Chalgrin to design the massive Roman-style **Arc de Triomphe** *(metro: Charles de Gaulle-Etoile; access by subway)* as a celebration of his military victories. Fifty metres (165ft) high and 45m (150ft) wide, it was still incomplete when the Emperor was toppled, and was finally finished only in 1836 under his nephew, Louis-

Philippe. At ground level are four high-relief sculptures, the finest of which, from the Champs-Elysées, are Rudes' *Departure of the Volunteers* in 1792, commonly known as the *Marseillaise* (right), and Cortot's *Triumph of 1810*, celebrating the Treaty of Vienna (left). The frieze above also depicts moments of Napoleonic glory, while the arch is inscribed with the names of 660 generals and 128 battles of the Empire. Beneath it lies the tomb of the Unknown Soldier. Stairs and a lift lead up to the roof, from where there are magnificent views. Inside is a small museum.

In 1854, Haussmann surrounded the Arc by a circle of twelve broad avenues, naming it the **Place de l'Etoile**. After de Gaulle's death in 1970 it was officially renamed **Place Charles de Gaulle**, but the name is rarely used.

AUTEUIL AND PASSY

Quiet, leafy and exclusive, the gilded great of Paris live firmly behind closed doors in this largely residential corner of Paris. Lively it is not, but it does have a number of small museums.

DON'T MISS

*** **The Arc de Triomphe:** less interesting than famous, you have to do it once.
*** **The Palais de Chaillot:** the museums are interesting but the views are superb.

Opposite: *Cherub riding a dolphin on the Pont Alexandre III.*
Left: *A symbol of France's battles, victories and freedom, the Arc de Triomphe is the starting point for the celebratory annual parade down the Champs-Elysées on 14 July.*

Right: *The Palais de Chaillot is built as two curved wings either side of a terrace and adorned with the work of many sculptors.*

Chief amongst them is the vast **Palais de Chaillot**, *place du Trocadéro, 16th (metro: Trocadéro)*, built for the 1937 Exhibition. The dramatic terraces in front of the building's hawk-like wings offer the best possible view of the Eiffel Tower as well as a perfect skateboard slalom course. Inside, the **Musée de la Marine** houses numerous models of famous French ships, as well as parts of the real thing, instruments and paintings.

Nearby, the **Musée des Arts Asiatiques Guimet**, *6 place d'Iéna, 16th (metro: Iéna)*, has a superb collection of Asian art, lush with ivory and temple bronzes, puppets and masks, Chinese porcelain and jade. The **Musée d'Art Moderne de la Ville de Paris**, in the Palais de Tokyo, *11 av du Président Wilson, 16th (metro: Alma-Marceau)*, kicks off triumphantly with Raoul Dufy's *La Fée Electricité*, the largest picture in the world, created, like the building itself, for the 1937 World Exhibition. Numerous other modern masters make this a fitting companion to the Pompidou Centre. The **Musée de la Mode et du Costume**, in the **Palais Galliera**, *10 av Pierre 1er de Serbie, 16th (metro: Iéna, Alma-Marceau)*, has some 16,000 costumes and textiles, shown in constantly changing exhibitions, to protect the fragile cloth. The **Musée Marmottan – Claude Monet**, *2 rue Louis-Boilly, 16th (metro: La Muette)*, is a family collection with many superb Monets and other Impressionists as well as medieval and Napoleonic furniture and art, and a magnificent collection of illuminated manuscripts.

OTHER MUSEUMS

Smaller museums include the **Fondation Le Corbusier**, *10 square du Docteur Blanche, 16th (metro: Jasmin)*, dedicated to the great architect; the **Maison de Balzac**, *47 rue Raynouard, 16th (metro: Passy, La Muette; RER: Kennedy-Radio-France)*, the novelist's home for seven years; the futuristic **Maison de Radio-France**, *116 av du Président-Kennedy, 16th (metro: Ranelagh)*, with exhibits about the history of French broadcasting, back to 1931; and the **Musée du Vin**, *rue des Eaux, 5 Square Charles Dickens, 16th (metro: Passy)*, with wax displays, tools and all you need to know about wine-making, in the 14th-century cellars of the old Abbey of Passy.

NORTH OF THE CHAMPS-ELYSEES

Another cluster of museums is centred on **Place St-Augustin**, with its huge 19th-century church and statue of Jeanne d'Arc. **Musée Jacquemart-André**, *158 boulevard Haussmann, 8th (metro: St-Philippe-du-Roule, Miromesnil)*, has a wonderful display of Italian Renaissance and 17th–18th century Flemish and French art. Look out for works by Donatello, Botticelli, Della Robbia, Tiepolo, Bernini, Rembrandt, Watteau, Boucher, Reynolds and Van Dyck. The **Musée Cernuschi**, *7 av Vélasquez, 8th (metro: Monceau, Villiers)*, concentrates solely on Chinese and Japanese art through the ages. The **Musée de Nissim de Camondo**, *63 rue Monceau, 8th (metro: Villiers, Monceau)*, has a superb collection of carpets, 18th-century furniture and *objets d'art*.

Further north still, at *59 av Foch, 16th (metro: Porte Dauphine)*, are the **Musée Arménien**, dedicated to Armenian arts, manuscripts and jewellery and the **Musée d'Ennery** of Far Eastern art, including a fine collection of Japanese netsukes. The **Musée de la Contrefaçon**, *16 rue de la Faisanderie, 16th (metro: Porte Dauphine)*, has a totally fascinating catalogue of fakes and forgeries, from 200BC to the present day. The **Musée des Lunettes et des Lorgnettes**, *2 av Mozart, 16th (metro: La Muette)*, has everything from spectacles to binoculars and is surprisingly interesting.

Below: *The 19th-century church of St Augustin was built on an iron framework by Baltard, who was also responsible for building the pavilions of Les Halles.*

7
The Eiffel Tower, Les Invalides and the Musée d'Orsay

Eiffel Tower ***

quai Branly (metro: Bir-Hakeim; RER: Champs-de-Mars, Tour Eiffel)

There are usually massive queues; arrive early and expect to wait. Wishing to mark the centenary of the Revolution in spectacular fashion, the organizers of the 1889 Exhibition looked at literally thousands of projects before settling, amidst a hail of protests, on engineer Gustave Eiffel's iron tower. Work began in 1887 and was completed in time for its official opening on 31 March 1889. The 320.75m (1051ft) high tower sits on four feet, forming a 125m (415ft) square so perfectly balanced that the pressure never exceeds more than 4kg per cm², the weight of a seated man. It weighs 9550 tonnes, contains 15,000 pieces of metal and 2.5 million rivets. There are 1652 steps to the third level (or, thankfully, you can ride Eiffel's original hydraulic lifts), from which, on a clear day, you can see up to 70km (45 miles). Originally it was painted in graduated colours, from a deep bronze at the base to a pale yellow at the top. In 1909, when Gustave Eiffel's highly profitable 20-year ticket concession came to an end, the tower received a last-minute reprieve from demolition in the interests of science. In 1914 it was commissioned as a transmitter, playing a vital role in the conduct of the war. In 1916 it became the beacon for the transatlantic radio-telephone service. Messages intercepted here led to the arrest of Mata Hari in February 1917. On 30 December 1921 it launched French civil broadcasting and in 1925 Citroën used it as the frame for the world's largest illuminated sign. Today, it is a meteorological and

PARIS

Eiffel Tower/Invalides   Seine

Boulevard Périphérique

DON'T MISS

*** **The Eiffel Tower**: 321m (1053ft) of iron railings.
*** **The Musée d'Orsay**: Monet, Van Gogh and other Impressionists' artworks.

Opposite: *A feat of engineering, the Eiffel Tower was erected in the Champ-de-Mars, scene of great jubilation on the Revolution's first anniversary.*

Opposite: *A gilded dome crowns the Eglise du Dôme of Les Invalides. Commissioned by Louis XIV, it became the burial place of Napoleon.*

aircraft navigation station, and television and radio transmitter. Little models of the metal monster are the single most popular souvenir of the city. Until 1930 it remained the tallest building in the world. A small museum on the first stage tells the story of the tower, including some of its most famous visitors and the numerous lunatic and often fatal stunts it has inspired. Above all, the tower has become the icon of Paris, an international symbol which

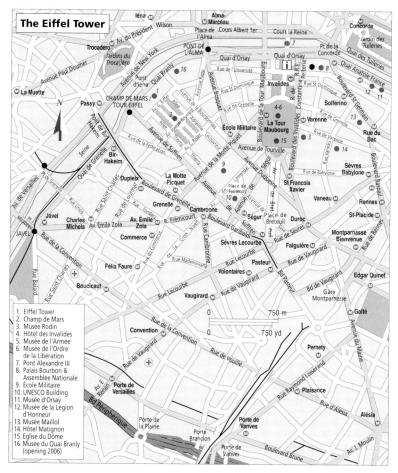

The Eiffel Tower

1. Eiffel Tower
2. Champ de Mars
3. Musée Rodin
4. Hôtel des Invalides
5. Musée de l'Armée
6. Musée de l'Ordre de la Libération
7. Pont Alexandre III
8. Palais Bourbon & Assemblée Nationale
9. École Militaire
10. UNESCO Building
11. Musée d'Orsay
12. Musée de la Légion d'Honneur
13. Musée Maillol
14. Hôtel Matignon
15. Eglise du Dôme
16. Musée du Quai Branly (opening 2006)

would surely gladden the hearts of that 1889 committee. In 2004, an ice-skating rink was suspended at the first level for Christmas. In 2006, a new museum, the Musée du Quai Branly (www.quaibranly.fr) is due to open, displaying the arts and civilizations of Africa, Oceania and the Americas.

Stretching back from the tower, the **Champ de Mars** began life as a military parade ground. In 1790 Louis XVI was reluctantly brought along to celebrate the first anniversary of the taking of the Bastille and in 1794 Robespierre held a massive festival here in honour of the Supreme Being and the immortality of the soul. Lighter entertainments have included balloon ascents, early flying machines, horse races and, during the Great Exhibitions, such diverse attractions as a train that ran on a cushion of water and a 70m (230ft) electric fairy. At the far end, the **École Militaire**, *13 place Joffre, 7th (metro: École Militaire)*, is an elegant and architecturally important Classical building designed by Jacques-Ange Gabriel in 1751, on the instigation of Madame de Pompadour. The aim of the military school was to train those with no money but good officer potential; its most famous graduate was Napoleon. Just behind this is the Y-shaped **UNESCO Building**, *7 place de Fontenoy, 7th (metro: Ségur, Cambronne)*, home of the United Nations Educational, Scientific, and Cultural Organization and an international treasure-trove of modern art, including works by Henry Moore, Miró, Le Corbusier and Picasso.

Hôtel des Invalides ★★

rue de Grenelle, 7th (metro: Varenne, Latour-Maubourg, Invalides).

Another huge ceremonial esplanade, laid out in 1720, leads from Pont Alexandre III (*see* page 72) to this massive complex, built in 1670–76 by Louis XIV as a veterans' hospital. Designed by Libéral Bruand, it centres on the **Cour d'Honneur**, inspired by the Escorial in Madrid, and housed 6000 men. On 14 July 1789 the mob broke in and stole 28,000 rifles, which they used in the attack on the Bastille. It was the first violent act of the Revolution. Behind the court, the **Eglise de St-Louis-des-Invalides** is

---

WALK

The lengthy Rue de l'Université runs from St-Germain-des-Prés to the Eiffel Tower. As you move west, the feeling changes from the bustling, villagey atmosphere of the Left Bank to the sophisticated and self-contained emotions of the chic 7th arrondissement. Street life gives way to the closed portes cochères of the grand hotels, many of which are now ministries or embassies.

The residential Rue St Dominique, between the Invalides and the Champ de Mars, is also a pleasant stroll with wonderful views of the Eiffel Tower. Small food shops are interspersed with clothes, flowers and household goods, and it is a good hunting ground for *dégriffés* garments. Look for the neo-classical Fontaine de Mars and, at no. 12, the wonderful Art Nouveau Liceo Italiano. Just off it, the well-heeled clientèle of the charming Rue Cler market is reflected in the quality of the merchandise.

hung with the flags and standards of France, and those captured from the enemy. The collection is thinner than it might have been; 1417 were incinerated by the governor in 1814, to save them from the clutches of the advancing Allies. The glittering gold **Eglise du Dôme** (1677–1735) was designed by Hardouin-Mansart as a royal chapel. Several military heroes of France are buried here, but they sink into obscurity beside the splendid **tomb of Napoleon**. He was buried here in 1840, 19 years after his actual death on St Helena, encased in six coffins, of iron, mahogany, lead (two), ebony, oak and the outer tomb of porphyry, surrounded by the names of his most famous victories. The tomb is viewed from the balcony, it is said, to ensure that you bow your head to the Emperor. Look for the stiff-necked Englishmen trying to peek without submitting!

The entrance to the **Musée de l'Armée** is marked by an old taxi, homage to the taxi drivers who ferried 7000 troops to the Battle of the Marne in 1914, saving Paris from invasion. This is one of the largest military collections in the world, with over 10,000 uniforms, including Henry II's armour, Napoleon's coat, military paintings and a seemingly endless supply of arms, many of artistic value. Look out for Napoleon's death mask; also his favourite dog and favourite horse, both stuffed. Still in Les Invalides, the **Musée des Plans-Reliefs** is a collection of beautiful scale models of fortified towns, started by Louis XIV in 1686. The last was added in 1870, but they remained an official secret until 1927.

Right: *Cannon on display at the Hôtel des Invalides. A military arsenal was kept here before the Revolution.*

Tucked behind a high wall, a few minutes' walk away, is the superb **Musée Rodin**, *77 rue de Varenne, 7th (metro: Varenne)*. Unlike so many of his contemporaries, Auguste Rodin (1840–1917) became such a success during his lifetime that he was offered the beautiful Hôtel Biron on condition that he left his work to the state. The resulting museum is small and immensely satisfying. The elegant salons and delightful gardens of the mansion built by Gabriel and Aubert (1731) are filled by a superb body of work by the master sculptor, including such famous pieces as *The Kiss*, *The Thinker*, *The Burghers of Calais* as well as the magnificent, harrowing *Gates of Hell*.

Above: *The iron-framed Gare d'Orsay has been converted into a light, spacious art gallery giving prominent display to the work of the Impressionists.*

The Rue de Varenne, which connects Invalides with the wealthy residential Faubourg-St-Germain, has a number of fine hotels, chief amongst them the **Hôtel Matignon** (no. 57), official residence of the Prime Minister. Just north on rue de Grenelle are the **Fontaine de Quatre Saisons**, carved by Bouchon between 1739 and 1745, and the **Musée Maillol** (*see* page 83).

Musée d'Orsay ★★★

1 rue de la Légion d'Honneur, 7th (metro: Solférino; RER: Musée d'Orsay)

The cavernous glass and iron Gare d'Orsay, built by Victor Laloux for the 1900 Exhibition, was once the most central of Paris's ring of railway stations. Saved at

Right: La Siesta *by Van Gogh (1853–1890) in the Musée d'Orsay. In 1886 the artist arrived in Paris, where he was influenced by the colours and attitudes of the Impressionist painters.*

IT'S A SCANDAL

When Manet's *Déjeuner sur l'Herbe* was exhibited at the Salon des Refusés in 1863 it caused a scandal. Based on Giorgione's *Concert champêtre*, Manet (1832–83) had produced a painting in the academic tradition in which he had trained, yet the official Salon rejected it. It was Manet's work, however, that inspired Monet and the other Impressionists, although Manet himself never exhibited with them. He continued to paint his subjects by emphasizing the contrast between light and dark tones, in which the use of black played an important part, rather than trying to convey his visual impressions. It was only late in his life that he took to painting outdoors and began using the 'rainbow palette' that excluded black.

---

the last minute from the crusher's ball, it re-opened in 1986, beautifully converted into a truly spectacular museum of art from 1848 to 1914, the period when Paris swept the world. A sculpture gallery runs through the heart of the museum, flanked by three floors of smaller galleries, showing the development of style from the ground up, with works by Ingres, Delacroix and Corot. The undoubted highlight is the magnificent Impressionist collection, which feels like the best sort of party, filled with old friends – from *Whistler's Mother* to the self-portraits by Cézanne and Van Gogh. Many of the world's most famous paintings are here, including Manet's *Olympia* and *Déjeuner sur l'Herbe*, which heralded the arrival of the Impressionist movement. Don't ignore some of the more unusual exhibits, including a room of delightful Toulouse-Lautrec pastels, furniture by Mackintosh and Frank Lloyd Wright, satirical sketches and an architecture gallery. If you only ever visit one museum, this must be the one.

A little way along the quay, the **Palais Bourbon**, *33 quai d'Orsay, 7th (metro: Assemblée-Nationale)*, stares across the river at the Place de la Concorde (*see page 69*). Built in 1722–8 for Louis XIV's daughter, the palace has a classical façade, added by Poyet on Napoleon's orders in 1807. Since 1827 it has been home to the French parliament, the Assemblée Nationale.

Left: Portrait *by Cézanne (1839–1906) in the Musée d'Orsay. Cézanne's work was exhibited at the first Impressionist exhibition in 1874.*

OTHER MUSEUMS IN THE AREA

The **Musée Maillol**, *59–61 rue de Grenelle, 7th* (*metro: rue du Bac*), focuses on the work of sculptor Aristide Maillol (1861–1944). Also includes works by other famous artists.

The **Musée de la Légion d'Honneur**, *2 rue Bellechasse, 7th* (*metro: Solférino; RER: Musée d'Orsay*), has a collection of military medals and decorations. It is named after Napoleon's highest order, inaugurated in 1802, and adjoins the **Palais de la Légion d'Honneur**. This 18th-century palace was built for a German prince who fell on hard times and was forced to sell the mansion and rent it as a tenant. After the Revolution it was raffled off. Later it was the home of Mme de Staël, whose salon became a focus for many of the intellectuals of the time.

The **Musée de l'Ordre de la Libération**, *51bis boulevard de Latour-Maubourg, 7th* (*metro: Latour-Maubourg*), commemorates the French during World War II, particularly the Free French and recipients of France's highest military honour, created by De Gaulle in 1940.

LES EXPOSITIONS UNIVERSELLES

In 1855, 1867, 1878, 1889, 1900, 1925 and 1937 Paris held a series of World Expositions which sent the city's reputation sparkling across the world and left it with a number of spectacular additions. Popular inventions promoted here included silver plate, the saxophone, the telephone, phonograph, television, an ice-making machine, and early automobiles … the list goes on and on. In 1855 Queen Victoria became the first British monarch to visit France since 1431. In 1889, the centenary of the Revolution, the star turn was the Eiffel Tower. In 1900 the exhibition created the flamboyant Pont Alexandre III, the Grand and Petit Palais (see page 71) and the Gare d'Orsay (see page 81).

8
The Rive Gauche and Montparnasse

St-Germain-des-Prés and Luxembourg

From the 7th century onwards, the area around St-Germain-des-Prés was totally dominated by its powerful Benedictine abbey, which remained effectively independent from the city, cultivating a sophisticated cosmopolitan atmosphere that survives until today. The development of the highly fashionable and expensive Faubourg St Germain assured it a place halfway between old money and radical chic. The Comédie Française flourished on the Rue de l'Ancienne Comédie until forced out by puritanical university officials in 1688 and the area had a famous month-long fair. In 1857 **Eugène Delacroix** set up his studio at 6 rue de Fürstenberg, now a small museum dedicated to the Romantic painter. Following World War II, the ever-mobile artists' colony, now led by the writers Sartre and de Beauvoir, moved north from Montparnasse (*see* page 93), settling into cafés like *Les Deux Magots*, *Brasserie Lipp*, *Café de Flore* and most historic of all, *Le Procope*, which claims to be the world's oldest coffee house, founded in 1686. Famous customers have included Voltaire, Oscar Wilde, Napoleon, Victor Hugo and Joseph Guillotin (1743–93), who perfected his killing machine on sheep in the nearby Cours de Rohan. Today, the area is filled with ultra-expensive apartments, trendy people, and the shops in which they love to spend their money. Its pavements are tarred because the students tore up the cobbles and hurled them at police during the May 1968 revolt, a fact commemorated in a pavement sculpture on Place St-Germain-des-Prés.

PARIS

Rive Gauche/
Montparnasse

Seine

Boulevard Périphérique

WALK

From Place St-Germain-des-Prés, walk down Rue Bonaparte, through Place St Sulpice, emerging on Rue de Vaugirard. Enter the Jardins du Luxembourg; leave on the far side, on Boulevard St Michel. Turn left, then right onto Rue Soufflot for the Panthéon. Walk back down Rue Soufflot. Halfway along, turn right onto Rue St Jacques. Turn left onto Rue des Ecoles and right onto Rue de Cluny for the Musée de Cluny; left for Boulevard St Germain. Cross and take Rue Boutebrie. At the top, turn left for Place St Michel and the metro.

Opposite: *Accordionist in the Latin Quarter.*

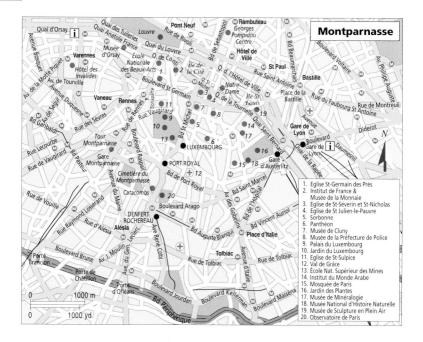

Montparnasse

1. Eglise St-Germain des Prés
2. Institut de France & Musée de la Monnaie
3. Eglise de St-Séverin et St-Nicholas
4. Eglise de St Julien-le-Pauvre
5. Sorbonne
6. Panthéon
7. Musée de Cluny
8. Musée de la Préfecture de Police
9. Palais du Luxembourg
10. Jardin du Luxembourg
11. Eglise de St-Sulpice
12. Val de Grâce
13. École Nat. Supérieur des Mines
14. Institut du Monde Arabe
15. Mosquée de Paris
16. Jardin des Plantes
17. Musée de Minéralogie
18. Musée National d'Histoire Naturelle
19. Musée de Sculpture en Plein Air
20. Observatoire de Paris

0 1000 m
0 1000 yd

The **Eglise St-Germain des Prés** opposite *(metro: St-Germain-des-Prés)* was founded by King Childebert in 542 to house several priceless relics, including a fragment of the True Cross, and was later named after the bishop of Paris at the time. Sacked four times by Normans in the 9th century, the earliest surviving sections date back to 866, making it the oldest church in Paris, although most of it was rebuilt in 1193. The abbey remained rich and powerful until the Revolution, when it was virtually destroyed and its priceless library confiscated. The mid-19th century restorers mangled a lot of what was left.

To the north, along the river, the **Musée de la Monnaie**, *11 quai de Conti, 6th (metro: St-Michel, Odéon)*, is housed in the old national mint, moved here by Louis XV in 1775. The museum, dedicated to cash, is surprisingly interesting and it is also possible to tour the medal workshops. Close by are the **Institut de France**, home to five academies of arts and sciences including the prestigious

Left: *In the square outside the church of St-Sulpice stands a fountain commemorating four French bishops – Bossuet, Fénelon, Massillon and Fléchier.*

Académie Française and the Académie des Sciences; and the **École Nationale des Beaux-Arts**.

To the south, work on the huge baroque **Eglise de St-Sulpice** *(place and metro: St-Sulpice)*, dedicated to a 7th-century archbishop of Bourges, began in 1646. Many architects, including Le Vau and Gittard, worked on it but the grandiose façade was added a century later by Florentine architect, Servandoni. The south tower was never finished. Inside are several fine 19th-century frescoes, including works by Delacroix, an 18th-century astronomical sundial, which marks the seasons and the hours of sunrise, and a magnificent organ (1781). In the square is the 1844 **Fontaine des Quatre Evêques**. Round

---

DON'T MISS

*** The Musée de Cluny**: the superb French National collection of medieval art, including the Lady and the Unicorn tapestries.
*** The Panthéon**: a cavernous former church full of heroes of France.
*** Latin Quarter**: cheerful alleys and cheap restaurants, oozing atmosphere.

Right: *Ponies wait patiently to give rides in a wintry Jardin du Luxembourg.*
Opposite: *A fresh seafood restaurant displays its delicacies in the Latin Quarter.*

the corner, on Rue de Sèvres, is one of the great department stores of Paris, **Le Bon Marché**.

A little further on is the **Jardin du Luxembourg**, *boulevard St Michel, 6th (RER: Luxembourg)*, formal gardens lined with benches and fine sculptures. Originally created for Marie de Medici in 1613, they were re-landscaped by Chalgrin in the 19th century. Today, they are a regular student hang-out. At the north end, perfectly reflected in a pond popular with model boaters is the **Palais du Luxembourg**, again built for Marie and heavily altered by Chalgrin. It is now home to the Senate and is only open for visits to the gallery when the house is sitting.

Below: *The Latin Quarter's twisting streets and alleys are a multi-cultural hive of activity and interest.*

THE LATIN QUARTER ★★★
(metro: St Michel, Maubert-Mutualité, Cluny-La Sorbonne)
On the other side of **Boulevard St Michel**, the main shopping street in the area, is a rare surviving fragment of medieval Paris, home to students since the 13th century. Rabelais nicknamed it because Latin was the only language used in the university grounds until the 19th century. Today, its huddle of narrow winding streets are filled with a multi-cultural cornucopia of cheap and cheerful cafés, kebab shops, crêperies, buskers and boutiques.

The **Eglise de St-Séverin et St-Nicholas**, *3 rue Prêtres-St-Séverin, 5th*, is the official university church, named after two 6th-century saints, both of whom did favours for King Clovis. Rebuilt at regular intervals from the 6th century onwards, the existing church is largely 15th-century Gothic, with several magnificent Romanesque capitals, a double ambulatory springing from a twisting central column, and some fine modern stained glass. The Rococo organ (1745) was played by Fauré and Saint-Saëns. In 1474 a condemned murderer was offered his freedom if he survived an experimental operation for gallstones. It was carried out in the garden, then a charnel-house. Astonishingly, the patient lived to tell the tale.

The little **Eglise de St-Julien-le-Pauvre**, *1 rue St-Julien-le-Pauvre, 5th*, was named after St Julian the Hospitaller who accidentally murdered his parents, and spent the rest of his life caring for the poor to make up for it. Built originally in the 6th century, it was largely rebuilt in the 13th century when it was used as an assembly hall for students. It was virtually destroyed during student riots in 1524, and rebuilt in 1651. Today, it is run by the Greek Orthodox Church.

Known universally as the Musée de Cluny, the **Musée National du Moyen Age**, *6 place Painlevé, 5th (metro: Cluny-La Sorbonne, St Michel, Odéon)* is housed in a magnificent mansion built *c*1500 by Jacques d'Amboise, Abbot of the Benedictine monastery founded here in the 1330s. Beside it are the **Thermes de Cluny**, 2nd-century AD Roman baths. Inside is the exquisite and superbly displayed national collection of medieval art and artefacts, founded by Alexandre de Sommerard in 1832. The state bought both the collection and the mansion in 1844. It is a

---

HOTEL DE CLUNY

The Hôtel de Cluny, which houses the museum of that name, is a fine example of a medieval domestic residence. The heraldic arms of the Amboise family surmount the archway that leads to its attractive courtyard and the house has had many illustrious inhabitants. The young Mary Tudor, sister of Henry VIII of England stayed here after the premature death of her much older husband, Louis XII of France. In the 17th century the mansion was the residence of the papal nuncios, including Mazarin.

Right: *The 15th-century Hôtel de Cluny is a fine example of a private mansion of the period and an appropriate setting for its superb collection of medieval art.*

Opposite: *The imposing 18th-century Panthéon is built in the classical style. Built as a church, it is the burial place of many of France's illustrious heroes.*

peerless treasure-trove of glittering gold crowns and reliquaries, smoothly rotund carvings in wood and ivory, glowing paintings, tapestries and stained glass, perfectly detailed illuminated manuscripts, stone capitals and heavy blackened furniture. In Salle VIII on the ground floor are the 28 heads of the Kings of Judea from Notre Dame (*see* page 35), beheaded in 1793 by Revolutionaries who believed them to be the kings of France. Salle XII, the barrel-vaulted frigidarium of the Roman baths, contains the 16th-century Grape Harvest Tapestry. Upstairs, in Salle XIII, the six sublime *millefleurs* tapestries depicting *La Dame à la Licorne* (The Lady and the Unicorn) were woven near Aubusson in the late 15th century and rescued from a dusty castle attic 400 years later. A medieval garden and *Forêt de la Licorne* (Unicorn Forest) based on the tapestries are situated north of the museum.

In about 1127 Peter Abélard and his followers gathered to debate in the open air; in 1215 the University of Paris was eventually given official recognition. In 1253 Robert de Sorbon, chaplain to St Louis, founded **La Sorbonne**, for 16 poor theology students. It grew almost overnight into one of the great universities of the world, housed today in a sprawl of 19th-century buildings, which stretch out behind the Rue des Ecoles and Boulevard St Michel.

Tucked in among them is the **Panthéon**, *place du Panthéon, 5th (metro: Luxembourg, Monge)*. The first abbey and church here was built in 508 by King Clovis, over St

Geneviève's tomb. In 1757, in payment of a vow, Louis XV began work on a new abbey church for the glory of France, the monarchy and St Geneviève. In the shape of a Greek cross, topped by a huge dome and fronted by a classical peristyle, it was designed by Soufflot and completed in 1789, just in time for the Revolution. In 1791 it became a Pantheon for the heroes of the Republic. In November 1793 Revolutionaries melted down the saint's reliquary, burnt her remains and scattered the ashes on the Seine. Over the next century it became a political football, turning from pantheon to church and back again several times before it finally became a civil building in 1885. Along the way, almost every major artist of the establishment of the 19th century had a hand in painting frescoes and carving sculptures depicting the life of St Geneviève, the heroes and saints of France, the civic virtues, and the glorious Revolution. Foucault, inventor of the gyroscope, carried out scientific experiments here in 1851–2, suspending a pendulum from the dome to prove the earth's rotary motion. Heroes of France buried here include Voltaire, Victor Hugo, Jean-Jacques Rousseau, Emile Zola, the architect Soufflot, Louis Braille (inventor of Braille), Jean Moulin (leader of the French Resistance in World War II), René Cassin (author of the United Nations Declaration of Human Rights), and economist Jean Monnet (a founder of the European Community). Marie Curie (1867–1934) was the first woman to be interred in the panthéon, reburied here in 1995.

Next door, the delightful little **Eglise de St-Etienne-du-Mont**, *place de l'Abbé Basset, 5th (metro: Luxembourg, Monge)*, was founded in 1492. The basic structure is Gothic, but the foundation stone for the portal was laid in 1610, and the enchant-ingly light façade and much of the interior, particularly the glorious rood screen and pulpit, are pure Renaissance. The few relics of St Geneviève

---

ST GENEVIEVE

Geneviève was a farmer's daughter, born in Nanterre in 422, who came to Paris and took holy orders. When Attila the Hun marched on the city in 451 Geneviève assured the terrified Parisians that they would be safe. When the Huns turned back without attacking her prophesy was hailed as a miracle. In 460 she built the first church over the tomb of St Denis (*see page 99*). On her death c509 her supposedly miraculous tomb became a popular place of pilgrimage and she was made patron saint of Paris, with her feast day on 3 January. The faithful prayed to her relics for three days before the Battle of the Marne in World War I and again the city was saved.

SMALL AND CURIOUS MUSEUMS

Collection Historique de la Préfecture de Police, *5 rue de la Montaigne Sainte Geneviève, (metro: Maubert-Mutualité)*. An often grisly collection of police instruments and famous clues.

Musée de l'Assistance Publique, *47 quai de la Tournelle, 5th (metro: Maubert-Mutualité)*. Paris's hospitals since the Middle Ages.

Musée Baccarat, *30 bis rue de Paradis (metro: Château d'Eau or Poissonière)*. Filled with beautiful pieces of crystal.

Musée de Curiosité et de la Magie, *11 rue St-Paul, 4th (metro: St Paul)*. Magic and illusion, complete with magic shows.

Musée de la Musique, *Cité de la Musique, 221 av Jean-Jaurès, 19th (metro: Porte de Plantin)*. The music museum displays a large collection of musical instruments.

Musée Jean Moulin, *23 allée de la 2e DB, 15th (metro: Montparnasse-Bienvenüe)*, dedicated to Jean Moulin (1899–1943), resistance leader during the World War II German occupation of Paris.

Musée du Vin, *Caveau des Echansons, rue des Eaux, 5 Square Charles Dickens, 16th (metro: Passy)*. Monastic cellars now devoted to the grape; tour includes tasting.

to survive the Revolution (including her finger) are now housed here as a focus of pilgrimage. The writers Pascal and Racine are buried here, as is the painter Le Sueur.

JARDIN DES PLANTES AREA

Stretched out along Quai St Bernard, the **Musée de Sculpture en Plein Air** *(metro: Jussieu, Monge)* is an open-air modern sculpture garden with works by Brancusi, Zadkine and César. A little further along, the fascinating **Institut du Monde Arabe**, *1 rue de Fossés St-Bernard, 5th (metro: Jussieu, Cardinal Lemoine)*, which opened in 1987, was designed by Jean Nouvel and paid for by the governments of France and 22 Islamic countries. Its windows, based on Islamic designs, have photo-electric panels that expand and contract like the pupil of an eye, according to the amount of available light. Inside is a superb museum of the Islamic world, with art, architecture, furniture, jewellery, and scientific and religious displays.

The **Jardin des Plantes** *(metro: Jussieu, Gare d'Austerlitz)* was originally laid out as a medicinal herb garden in 1626 by Jean Hérouard and Guy de la Brosse, court physicians to Louis XIII. They also founded schools of botany, natural history and pharmacy which have mutated into a magnificent botanical garden. Buffon, the naturalist, was superintendent here in 1739–88. Inside, the **Musée National d'Histoire Naturelle**, *57 rue Cuvier, 5th (metro: Gare d'Austerlitz)*, is filled with fossilized plants, dinosaur bones, and lumps of rock.

In 1791 the last four surviving animals from the Versailles menagerie were moved into the garden. The collection has grown, although most of the zoo's inhabitants were eaten during the 1870–1 siege. Today, it is a pleasant little **zoo**, with large cats, bears and a wide variety of small animals and creepy-crawlies.

Behind the park the 1926 **Mosquée de Paris**, *place du Puits-de-l'Ermite, 5th (metro: Monge)*, was built as a memorial to the Muslims who died in World War I. Today it is the cultural and religious headquarters of almost 5 million French Muslims. The fine courtyard is modelled on the Alhambra.

Also nearby is the 2nd-century AD Roman **Arènes de Lutèce**, *rue des Arènes, 5th (metro: Cardinal Lemoine, Jussieu)*. The arena was destroyed by barbarians, rediscovered in 1869, and largely reconstructed in 1917.

MONTPARNASSE AND THE SOUTH

Montparnasse started life as a slag heap from the Roman quarries, nicknamed Mount Parnassus by students who gathered here for wine, women and poetry. From about 1800 onwards it attracted an increasingly large number of cafés and cabarets, but it really took off in the early 20th century as rents in Montmartre soared and the penniless artistic and intellectual community moved here en masse. Lenin, Trotsky, Hemingway, Gertrude Stein, Picasso and Eisenstein all worked and drank here. Tourists still flock to the area to breathe in the air of genius, but usually find only petrol fumes. The artists moved to St-Germain after the war and in the 1960s the area became the site of some horrendous 'new town' planning. Several of the famous cafés of the past survive, including **Le Select**, **Le Dôme**, **La Rotonde**, and **La Coupole**, where 30 artists contributed to the décor. Infinitely more expensive now, they are havens of warmth in a cold and uninviting concrete jungle.

At the heart of the new development soars the gigantic **Tour Maine-Montparnasse**, *rue de l'Arrivée, 15th (metro: Montparnasse-Bienvenue)*; the tallest building in France, at 210m (700ft). There is a closed viewing platform on the 56th floor, and an open one on the 59th. On a clear day you can see up to 40km (25 miles). Post your cards here for a Tour Montparnasse frank.

Those interested in more than a mere postmark should visit the **Musée de la Poste**, *34 boulevard de Vaugirard, 15th (metro: Montparnasse-Bienvenue)*, which has a magnificent stamp collection, and

Below: *It may look uninspiring, but the Tour Maine-Montparnasse offers a superb view of Paris and its environs.*

Jean-Paul Sartre and Simone de Beauvoir were life-long companions and two of the most influential thinkers of the 20th century. Sartre created the philosophy of Existentialism, which states that existence is basically futile, with no great purpose or meaning. You are totally free to mould and give value to your own life. Simone de Beauvoir's seminal work on the role of women, *The Second Sex* (1949), helped shape the thinking of the early Feminist movement and create a worldwide social revolution. Both were also highly entertaining writers, with a string of successful novels and plays.

LIBERTY

The US Statue of Liberty in New York Harbour, properly called 'Liberty Enlightening the World', was given by France to the people of the USA to commemorate the centenary of American independence in 1876. Bartholdi's massive statue stands 67m (220ft) high, but a much smaller version of it can be seen in Paris at the extremity of the Île des Cygnes in the midst of the river Seine, downstream past the Pont de Grenelle.

traces the history of the post from medieval parchments to the balloons and carrier pigeons used by besieged Parisians to relay messages in 1870.

Nearby, the **Cimetière de Montparnasse**, *3 boulevard Edgar Quinet, 14th (metro: Edgar-Quinet)*, is the third largest cemetery in Paris, founded in 1824. Its famous permanent residents include writers Jean-Paul Sartre (1905–80), Simone de Beauvoir (1908–86), Samuel Beckett (1906–89), Charles Baudelaire (1821–67) and Guy de Maupassant (1850–93); composers César Franck (1822–90) and Camille Saint-Saëns (1835–1921); sculptors Antoine Bourdelle (1861–1929), Ossip Zadkine (1890–1967), François Rude (1784–1855) and Frédéric Bartholdi (sculptor of the Statue of Liberty) (1834–1904); and André Citroën, founder of the car company.

For centuries, Parisian corpses were shoe-horned into a tiny corner of Les Halles (*see* page 40), but the body count rose out of control. In 1780 several people were asphyxiated by the smell. Something had to be done. Work began in 1785. It took 15 months to transfer an estimated two million bodies from the central cemeteries to an ancient quarry, which became known as the **Catacombs**, *1 place Denfert-Rochereau, 14th (metro: Denfert-Rochereau)*. Bones were stacked neatly on shelves, and skulls arranged in artistic heaps. The tourists flocked in; the aristocracy held parties and concerts; and the Resistance set up their headquarters in this unlikely place during World War II.

Nearby, the **Observatoire de Paris**, *av de l'Observatoire, 14th (metro: Denfert-Rochereau)*, was founded by Louis XIV in 1667 for the Académie des Sciences. It was designed by Claude Perrault on aesthetic rather than scientific principles, and early astronomers had to set up the telescope in the garden. It nevertheless became an important scientific centre, responsible for creating the metric system, discovering Neptune and calculating the exact circumference of the earth, the distance of the earth from the sun and the speed of light. Until 1884 it was the home of the Paris meridian, which vied with Greenwich as 0° longitude.

Left: *The Fontaine de l'Observatoire was designed by Davioud in 1873. Its magnificent rearing horses were sculptured by Frémiet.*

It is still home to the Coordinated Universal Clock, official measure of French time.

The **Manufacture des Gobelins**, *42 av des Gobelins, 13th (metro: Gobelins)*, the famous Gobelins tapestry works, was founded in the early 17th century in an old dyeing factory. In 1662 Louis XIV annexed it and as a royal institution it became world renowned. At the same time the Gobelins took over the running of the royal carpet factory whose premises were a soapworks at Chaillot. Today you can watch workers manufacture traditional and modern designs and repair the priceless works of their forebears.

Further southeast, Tolbiac was chosen as the new site for the **Bibliothèque Nationale de France**, *11 quai François Mauriac, 13th (metro: Quai de la Gare)*. Commissioned by President Mitterrand, the four distinctive towers house not only the country's most prestigious library, but also reading rooms, exhibition rooms and a restaurant.

LES GOBELINS

The Gobelins factory is a fascinating place to visit and guided tours take you through the whole process and weaving of these magnificent tapestries. Artist-weavers undergoing study live on the premises and follow a long and thorough course of training in all aspects of weaving, dyeing and design. The tapestries are woven on looms, working from the reverse. The design to be followed is placed behind the weaver and the image is copied from its reflection in a mirror. Many of the designs are the work of well-known artists and the colour matching of yarn to paint is perfect. The tapestries now are mostly woven commissions to be given as diplomatic gifts by the French government.

9
The Suburbs

Bois de Boulogne ★★

(metro: Porte Maillot, Porte Dauphine, Porte d'Auteuil, Sablons; not safe at night).

Covering a massive 845ha (2085 acres), the Bois de Boulogne was a hunting preserve before it was enclosed in 1558 as a royal park. It became highly fashionable as a promenade and duelling ground when Louis XV opened it to the public, but it was only in 1852 that Baron Haussmann created a fully fledged public park after Napoleon III gave the area to the city. The Bois was inspired by London's Hyde Park, with winding walks. There are several distinct areas. The children's **Jardin d'Acclimation** has a playground, petting zoo, miniature railway, giant doll's house, bowling alley and an art gallery and Internet workshop, the **Musée en Herbe**. The **Musée National des Arts et Traditions Populaires**, next door, has a fine rural crafts collection. The **Pré Catalan**, named after a 12th-century Provençal minstrel murdered there, has a magnificent copper beech and the Jardin de Shakespeare, of plants mentioned in his plays. There are also two large boating lakes and particularly fine formal gardens in the **Jardin des Serres d'Auteuil** and the **Parc de Bagatelle**, which surrounds a delightful house built in 64 days in 1775 as a bet between Marie-Antoinette and the Comte d'Artois.

The most famous of the many amateur and professional sporting facilities are the **Roland Garros tennis stadium**, home of the French Open, and **Longchamps** (flat) and **Auteuil** (jump) racecourses.

Don't Miss

★★★ **The Grande Arche de la Défense**: latest in a long line of monumental arches.
★★★ **Malmaison**: the Empress Josephine's delightful château and rose garden.

Opposite: *The Bois de Boulogne offers an area of rural beauty and relaxation within a short distance of the centre of Paris.*

Above: *The Grande Arche de la Défense.*

LA DÉFENSE

A huge rebuilding programme planned to revitalize the inner suburbs, has taken place since the 1960s. The centre-piece, the **Grande Arche de La Défense** *(RER Line A: Grande Arche de la Défense)* is a gleaming white 100m (330ft) cube. It was designed by Danish architect, Johann-Otto von Sprekelsen and inaugurated in 1989 to celebrate the Bicentennial of the Revolution. The sculptural canopy of 'clouds' is the work of British engineer Peter Rice. The views from the top are excellent. The multimedia information centre in the base of the arch has a wealth of information relating to Europe and the European Union.

A small museum at the **Info-Défense** tourist office *(15 place de la Défense)* has an interesting display of architectural plans, models and projects regarding the development of La Défense.

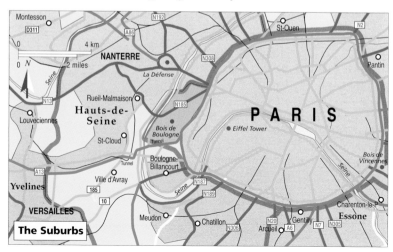

Left: *19th-century Viollet-le-Duc carefully restored the Benedictine basilica of St Denis.*

LA DÉFENSE

La Défense is named after the 1870–71 defence of Paris. Work began on this ultra-modern business park, the largest construction project since the Maginot Line, in 1955. Designed to preserve the city centre from over-development, it has become a vast, soulless open esplanade, surrounded by tower blocks. Many were considered revolutionary in their day. Sadly, all too many now look tired, although some of the buildings and many of the scattered sculptures, by artists such as Miró and Calder, are interesting. About 35,000 people live here, and 130,000 work in its many offices.

MOBILE MARTYR

In AD262 St Denis, first bishop of Paris, finally went too far, desecrating several statues of Roman gods and emperors. He was arrested and beheaded on the Mont de Mercure (later renamed Montmartre in his honour). Defiant beyond the end, he picked up his head, tucked it under one arm, and strode off down the road. He finally stopped and was buried some 6km (4 miles) north, near the village of Catoliacus. St Denis is the patron saint of France.

ST-DENIS
Basilique de St-Denis *
place de la Légion d'Honneur (metro: St-Denis-Basilique).

As soon as St Geneviève built the first chapel over the tomb of St Denis in the 5th century, it became a popular pilgrimage centre. In the 7th century King Dagobert sponsored the foundation of a great royal abbey, which became the traditional burial place of kings. In about 1135 Abbot Suger began work on a stunning new church, the first Gothic structure in France, completed by Pierre de Montreuil in the 13th century. Henry IV pragmatically renounced his Protestant beliefs here in 1593 in order to claim the throne of France. During the Revolution the church was desecrated and the royal corpses dumped in

Above: *The tombs of the kings of France in the basilica of St Denis.*

Opposite: *Detail from a tile in the Musée National de la Céramique, Sèvres.*

Below: *Malmaison became Josephine's home after her divorce from Napoleon.*

a communal grave. Astonishingly, the 79 tombs survived. Viollet-le-Duc restored the basilica in the 19th century.

The excellent **Musée d'Art et d'Histoire**, *22bis rue Gabriel Péri*, is a 17th-century Carmelite convent with a fine art collection, including modern masterpieces, apothecaries' tools, local archaeology and a fascinating display on the 1871 Paris Commune. Thanks to the highly publicized 1998 World Cup final (when France beat Brazil to immense national pride) in the **Stade de France** *(RER line D to Stade de France St-Denis)*, St-Denis has been firmly placed on the map. Apart from sporting events, the 100,000-seat Stade is also used to stage concerts and shows and can be toured.

OTHER SIGHTS

Malmaison *(RER line A to La Défense, then bus 158 to Bois Préau)*. In 1800 Napoleon and Josephine, aided by architects Percier and Fontaine, began to transform a rather ramshackle house into a residence fit for a Consul of France. The enchanting château became Josephine's main residence after her divorce in 1809. The house is a fascinating record of the heyday of the Empire. Redouté,

whose charming paintings of roses adorn the château, was among the staff who cherished Josephine's precious rose gardens. The **Château de Bois-Préau**, *1 Ave de l'Impératrice*, next door, houses a Napoleonic museum.

From the 11th century the **Bois de Vincennes** (*metro: Porte Dorée, Château de Vincennes*) was a royal hunting preserve. It became a military firing range in 1796 and a huge, supposedly English-style, park in 1860. Today it is Paris' largest park at 995ha (2460 acres). The iris gardens are fabulous in season, but there is a general lack of interesting plants. To make up for this, there is a huge zoo and boating on Lake Daumesnil.

The no-nonsense **Château de Vincennes** (1337–80) comprises a solid keep and 15th–16th century copy of the Sainte-Chapelle (*see* page 32), surrounded by a formidable curtain wall and moat. In the early 17th century Le Vau added a new Résidence Royale, but Louis XIV turned the fortress into a prison. The castle has a colourful history – Henry V of England died in the keep, the Marquis de Sade and Mirabeau were imprisoned here and Mata Hari was shot here. Fouquet, who built Vaux-le-Vicomte (*see* page 110), and upset Louis XIV, was also incarcerated here. There are small museums on the château's history, military insignia and mountaineering.

The fascinating **Musée des Arts d'Afrique et d'Océanie**, *293 av Daumesnil*, was built for the 1931 Exhibition as a celebration of the French colonies, but now houses a much wider anthropological collection from across Africa and the Pacific, and a tropical aquarium.

St Cloud and Sèvres, 10km (6 miles) west of Paris (*metro: Pont de Sèvres, Boulogne-Pont de St Cloud*). Only Le Nôtre's delightful gardens, with their panoramic views of Paris and tumbling Grand Cascade of water terraces remain; Hardouin-Mansart's château (1675) was burnt to a crisp during the 1870 Siege of Paris. Napoleon staged his coup here on 9 November 1799. On the edge of the park are the **Manufacture de Sèvres**, home of fine porcelain since the 18th century, and the **Musée National de la Céramique**, *place de la Manufacture*, with thousands of ceramics from across the globe.

OTHER SIGHTS OF INTEREST

Le Centre Internationale de l'Automobile, *25 rue d'Estienne d'Orves, Pantin (metro: Hoche – Line 5)*. An enthusiast's dream collection of 100 cars. Famous motoring names include Ferrari, Ascari, Fangio and Jim Clark.
Le Château de Sceaux, 10km (6 miles) southwest of Paris *(RER Line B to Bourg-la-Reine)*. This mid-19th century pastiche of a château is home to the **Musée de l'Île de France**. Le Nôtre's 17th-century gardens are magnificent.
Musée de l'Air et de l'Espace, *Le Bourget (RER Line B to Le Bourget or bus 350 from Gare de l'Est and Gare du Nord)*. Fascinating air museum with a collection of nearly 180 aircraft, at one of the world's great historic airports.
La Roseraie de l'Hay-les-Roses *(RER Line B to Bourg-la-Reine, then bus 192)*. The ultimate rose garden, created in 1892, with over 3500 species in 5km (3 miles) of flower beds.

10
The Île de France

Disneyland Paris ★★★

A miniature version of its American parents but growing fast, Disneyland is visited by over 12.5 million people each year. Five themed areas cluster round the towering spires of **Sleeping Beauty's Castle**. Start early and you can get round everything in one day.

Vintage cars and horse-drawn carriages ply **Main Street, USA** – small town East Coast America *c*1900 – which is also the route of the daily grand parades (usually late afternoon). Don't buy all your souvenirs in this concentration of shops and eateries, as each area has its own themed merchandise. Above the main entrance is the first of four stations of the **Disneyland Railroad**, a little steam train which chugs round the edge of the park.

Frontierland is yee-ha Wild West, with a Mark Twain riverboat steamer, a ghostly mansion, shooting gallery, and the scream-making Big Thunder Mountain roller-coaster among the rides and attractions.

In **Adventureland** are the Temple of Doom roller-coaster, tree-top home of the Swiss Family Robinson, an adventure island complete with rope walkways, Pirates of the Caribbean and Aladdin's Cave.

The cutely pastelled **Fantasyland**, home of Mickey, Pluto et al, is heartland of the Disney ideal and the best area for small children, with rides on Dumbo, giant teacups, ferris wheel, toy train and merry-go-round, and gentle cruises through the fairy tales, past the children of the world, and the enchanting stories of Pinocchio, Snow White and Peter Pan.

OTHER THEME PARKS

France Miniature, Elancourt *(RER Line C to St-Quentin-en-Yvelines, then bus no. 411)*. A giant map of France with waist-high miniatures of the country's top historical monuments and typical villages. **Parc Astérix**, Plailly *(RER Line B3 to Aéroport Charles de Gaulle 1 station, then a shuttle bus)*. Popular theme park based on the cartoon adventures of Astérix the Gaul. While Disneyland is very popular, the patriotic French still have a soft spot for Astérix.

Opposite: *Meet Goofy at Disneyland Paris.*

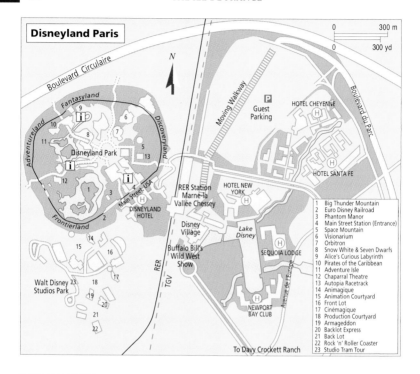

Disneyland Paris

0	300 m
0	300 yd

1	Big Thunder Mountain
2	Euro Disney Railroad
3	Phantom Manor
4	Main Street Station (Entrance)
5	Space Mountain
6	Visionarium
7	Orbitron
8	Snow White & Seven Dwarfs
9	Alice's Curious Labyrinth
10	Pirates of the Caribbean
11	Adventure Isle
12	Chaparral Theatre
13	Autopia Racetrack
14	Animagique
15	Animation Courtyard
16	Front Lot
17	Cinémagique
18	Production Courtyard
19	Armageddon
20	Backlot Express
21	Back Lot
22	Rock 'n' Roller Coaster
23	Studio Tram Tour

DISNEYLAND FACTS

32 km (19 miles) east of Paris on the A4-E50; RER Line A4 to Marne-la-Vallée/ Chessy. Entrance 'passport' lasts 1, 2 or 3 days or 1 day; children aged 2 and under free; child rate for 3–11 year olds. All rides and attractions included. Strollers and wheelchairs for hire by the entrance. Go to City Hall, Main Street, to find lost children or property or to leave messages. First Aid and baby care facilities in Central Plaza. For information, phone Guest Relations, tel: 01 60 30 60 23 or 01 60 30 60 30.

The park's newest attraction, **Walt Disney Studios**, brings film, animation and television production to life with a *Sunset Boulevard* sound stage, a production back-lot and animation studios.

Festival Disney provides themed evening entertainment, food and drink outside the main park. There is also a spectacular **Buffalo Bill Wild West Show** and barbecue every evening.

VERSAILLES ***

RER Line C5 to Versailles-Rive Gauche. Arrive early to beat the tour buses; plan carefully as different sections of the buildings open at different times and wear comfortable shoes for lots of walking. Allow time to visit the extensive gardens as well as the château.

Until 1661, when Fouquet was unwise enough to be

more glamorous than the king (*see* page 110), Versailles was a simple hunting lodge. But Louis XIV really believed himself to be little short of divine and wanted a palace to match – bigger, better, more lavish and luxuriant than anyone else's. It took only 21 years for the architects Le Vau and Hardouin-Mansart to complete a palace whose sheer size, with its 580m (1900ft) long façade, leaves you gasping, although it was stripped of its furniture during the Revolution and many of the grandiose rooms are still very bare. While you wonder at the elaborate décor, you need imagination to repopulate this most glamorous of courts with up to 20,000 people including royalty, attendant aristocracy, government, foreign visitors, servants and even sightseers; anyone presentable was allowed to wander through and have a look, while the king got up and ready for bed in public and the poor queen even had her children with an audience.

The Château

Louis XIII's original lodge is just visible at the back of the **Cour de Marbre**, totally engulfed by the enormous wings. In the north wing are the sumptuous *faux marbre* private theatre, the **Opéra Royal**, finished in 1770 for the wedding of Louis XVI and Marie-Antoinette, Robert de

---

THE SUN KING

Louis XIV (1643–1715) came to the throne in 1643, aged five, with his mother, Anne of Austria, as regent, but only to power after the death of Cardinal Mazarin in 1661. In 1660 he married Infanta Maria Theresa of Spain. He spent 38 years at war with Spain, the Netherlands, Alsace, southern Germany and Italy while his Chief Minister, Colbert, enforced endless pernickety laws, creating a total dictatorship. Above all, Louis is remembered as the flamboyant 'Sun King' who thought himself divine, identified with Apollo, created a glittering era of lavish spending and great art, and bled the country dry.

Below: *The site of Versailles was originally marshland; 30,000 workers had to level and drain the area.*

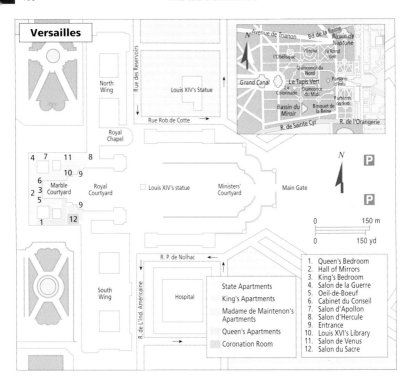

Versailles

North Wing
Rue des Reservoirs
Louis XIV's Statue
Royal Chapel
Rue Rob.de Cotte

Avenue de Trianon   Bd de la Reine   Bassin de Neptune
l'Obelisque   l'Etoile   le Rond Vert
Grand Canal   Quinconce du Nord   Le Tapis Vert   Parterre d'eau
La Colonnade   Quinconce du Midi
Bassin du Miroir   Bosquet de la Reine   Parterres du Sud
R. de Sainte Cyr   R. de l'Orangerie

4 7   11   8
10 9
6
2 3   Marble Courtyard   Royal Courtyard
5
9
1   12
Louis XIV's statue
Ministers' Courtyard
Main Gate

South Wing
R. de L'Ind. Américaine
R. P. de Nolhac
Hospital

0   150 m
0   150 yd

State Apartments
King's Apartments
Madame de Maintenon's Apartments
Queen's Apartments
Coronation Room

1. Queen's Bedroom
2. Hall of Mirrors
3. King's Bedroom
4. Salon de la Guerre
5. Oeil-de-Boeuf
6. Cabinet du Conseil
7. Salon d'Apollon
8. Salon d'Hercule
9. Entrance
10. Louis XVI's Library
11. Salon de Venus
12. Salon du Sacre

Le Nôtre

André Le Nôtre (1613–1700) was the foremost French landscape gardener of the 17th century. Responsible for the gardens at Vaux-le-Vicomte, he was commissioned by Louis XIV to design the superb grounds of Versailles. Here he planned a masterpiece series of formal outdoor 'rooms', placing them against a backdrop of natural wooded areas, as an appropriate setting for the vast palace.

Cotte's beautiful creamy baroque **Chapelle Royale** (1710), and the elaborately gilded and decorated **Grands Appartements**, each dedicated to one of the Roman gods. The Salon d'Apollon was the throne room; the Salon de Mercure, the state bedroom; the Salon de Diane a games room; and the Salon de Mars a ballroom. All are heavily embellished. By far the most magnificent is the glittering 75m (250ft) long **Galerie des Glaces** (Hall of Mirrors), with 17 vast windows carefully arranged so that the sun's dazzling light would reflect off the mirrors and back outside, to make it seem as if the Sun King really did shine. It was here, in the aftermath of the Franco-Prussian War, that Bismarck made the Kaiser head of a united Germany, and here, in November 1919, that Germany signed the Treaty of Versailles, officially ending World War I.

From 1727 onwards, Louis XV, together with Jacques-Ange Gabriel, began to create the **Petits Cabinets**, charming rooms on a more human scale, which became the apartments of his powerful mistress, Madame du Barry. In 1738 he himself moved from the chilly state bedroom into a new suite of **Appartements du Roi**, filled with magnificent carvings by Verberkt. The **Appartements de la Reine**, designed originally for Marie Leczinska in 1729, were in the south wing. They are now furnished as they would have been for Marie-Antoinette.

Don't Miss

*** **Versailles**: Louis XIV's palace of palaces.
*** **Disneyland Paris**: Disney's attempt to outstrip Louis XIV.

The Grounds

The magnificent gardens, restored to Le Nôtre's original 17th-century splendour, are vast. Directly in front of the château is a formal patterned terrace of lawns, fountains and pathways, studded by some 200 magnificent statues, many of which used to be gilded. Beyond this stretch the Grand and Petit Canals, which once had their own fleet of boats including gondolas and an orchestral barge, conducted by Lully.

To the right is the **Grand Trianon**. The first pavilion here was built as a trysting place where Louis XIV could meet his mistress, Madame de Montespan. The current building by Mansart (1687) became a private inner court to which only intimates and the highly favoured were invited. Carefully restored, it is now the most lavishly decorated of all the palace suites, giving a clear vision of the sumptuous life at court.

Below: *The ornate, lavishly gilded and rather public bedroom of the 'Sun King' Louis XIV at Versailles.*

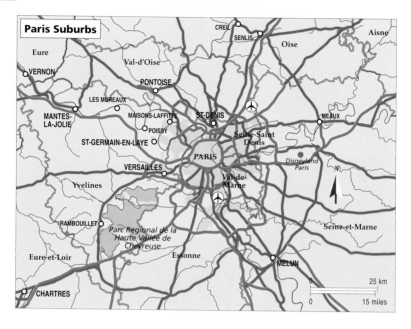

Paris Suburbs

CREIL
SENLIS
Oise
Aisne
Eure
Val-d'Oise
VERNON
PONTOISE
LES MUREAUX
MANTES-LA-JOLIE
MAISONS-LAFFITTE
ST-DENIS
MEAUX
POISSY
Seine-Saint Denis
ST-GERMAIN-EN-LAYE
PARIS
Disneyland Paris
N
VERSAILLES
Val-de-Marne
Yvelines
RAMBOUILLET
Parc Regional de la Haute Vallée de Chevreuse
Seine-et-Marne
Eure-et-Loir
Essonne
MELUN
CHARTRES
0   25 km
0   15 miles

OTHER SIGHTS OF INTEREST

L'Abbaye de Royaumont, Asnières-sur-Oise, 35km (22 miles) north of Paris. A beautifully preserved Cistercian abbey, founded by the saintly king Louis in 1228.
Musée de la Photographie, Bièvres (RER C to Massy-Palaiseau, then bus 2002 to Serinet). A Frenchman invented photography. This vast, exhaustive collection of 15,000 cameras is a suitable tribute.

Another royal mistress, Madame de Pompadour, kept Louis XV entertained from 1745–9, by building the New Menagerie, a glamorous farmyard centred on the **Pavillon Français**. In 1761 botanical gardens were laid out in the surrounding area, though later changed to the less formal English style preferred by Marie-Antoinette.

In 1763 work began on the **Petit Trianon**, an almost perfect, deceptively simple little classical palace, designed by Jacques-Ange Gabriel. Louis XVI gave this to his charming and frivolous wife, Marie-Antoinette (1755–93) who spent her happiest moments here with a small, informal group of intimates. She also spent vast amounts of money remodelling the surrounding gardens into artificial countryside, and building a model village and farmhouse, the **Hameau**, where she and her ladies-in-waiting would wander dressed as milkmaids. Labourers were employed for the real farm work at the dairy and mill. The queen was near here when the Revolutionary mob attacked the palace.

OTHER SIGHTS
Fontainebleau ***

65km (40 miles) southeast of Paris (SNCF from Gare de Lyon to Fontainebleau-Avon, then bus)

Louis the Fat (1108–37) first declared this area a royal hunting preserve and a vast and exceptionally beautiful forest still surrounds the town. In 1527, however, François I demolished the old fortress and commissioned the architect Gilles le Breton to build him the delightful Renaissance château which is the prime attraction. A favourite palace for generations of rulers, almost every future monarch added, demolished and altered bits of it. During the Revolution, it was stripped bare, the canal was drained and the fish were sold to the masses. Nevertheless, it is one of the most charming palaces in France, with a real sense of history and continuity. Napoleon loved Fontainebleau and spent much of his time here. He signed his abdication on 6 April 1814 in the dramatically named Cour des Adieux. The **Musée Napoléonien d'Art et d'Histoire Militaire** concentrates on his daily life.

Below: *The beautiful cathedral of Chartres is justly famed for its fine stained-glass windows, especially for the clear 'Chartres blue' colour.*

Chartres **

88km (55 miles) southwest of Paris (SNCF from Gare Montparnasse to Chartres)

Like Notre Dame, the magnificent cathedral at Chartres stands on ground sacred to many religions over thousands of years. The earliest Christian church was built in the 4th century. It became a major pilgrimage centre in 876 when Charlemagne's grandson, Charles the Bald, presented the Sancta Camisia, supposedly the cloth worn by Mary while giving birth to Christ. The crypt of the existing cathedral dates to 1024, while the

OTHER CHATEAUX

Dampierre, *Dampierre-sur-Boutonne-Yvelines, 36km (21 miles) southwest of Paris*. A dignified 17th-century brick and stone château, surrounded by formal flower gardens. **Ecouen** *20km (12¹/₂ miles) north of Paris (metro Line 13 to St-Denis Porte de Paris, then bus 268C, or SNCF from Gard du Nord to Ecouen-Ezanville)*. A supremely elegant early 16th-century château, which now houses the lavish **Musée Nationale de la Renaissance**. **Milly-la-Forêt**, *50km (31 miles) south of Paris*. The highlight is the nearby **Château de Courances**, with its magnificent 17th-century gardens, but the delightful village has several small exhibitions dedicated to local painters (Rousseau, Decamps, Daubigny and Millet) and an audio-visual on the poet Jean Cocteau.

ECLIPSING THE SUN

In 1661 Fouquet invited the Sun King and court to a grand fête to celebrate the opening of his superb new château, Vaux-le-Vicomte. Louis became so sick with jealousy that he arrested its owner, stripped him of office, possessions and title and exiled him for life. He then set to work to build something much bigger and better. The result was Versailles.

spectacular Gothic church, soaring above the little town, was built in the early 13th century. Above all, it has 172 peerless 13th-century stained-glass windows, telling stories of heroes and the Bible, showing the lives of peasants and princes, honouring God, the saints and the people who paid for them in a unique record of medieval life and thought. Even the local merchants donated 42 windows, each showing the speciality of the guild. The narrow streets around the cathedral have many delightful half-timbered buildings, several other fine churches and a Musée des Beaux-Arts.

St-Germain-en-Laye *
18km (11 miles) west of Paris (RER Line A)
The first castle on this wooded site overlooking the Seine was built in 1124. The earliest surviving building is St Louis' delicate 13th-century Sainte-Chapelle. The surviving château, the work of François I, belongs to the Renaissance, but there was another later version built by Philibert d'Orme in 1557, of which only the Pavillon Henri IV remains. Louis XIV was born here, escaped back here from the mob during the Fronde rebellion and set up court for nearly 40 years, until Versailles was complete. Since 1855 the château has been home to the **Musée des Antiquités Nationales**, the national archaeology collection. The former 17th-century Hôpital Général Royal, *2bis rue Maurice Denis*, now houses the important **Musée Maurice Denis**, dedicated to the artist and his friends, with works by Gauguin, Bonnard, Vuillard, Mondrian and Lalique.

Vaux-le-Vicomte *
55km (34 miles) southeast of Paris (SNCF from Gare de Lyon to Melun, then taxi)
This magnificent château was built by Le Vau for Louis XIV's finance minister, Fouquet, in 1661. The entire project was undertaken in five years. Lavishly ornamented, with frescoes by Le Brun in the Grand Salon, and fine gardens by Le Nôtre, it is acknowledged to be one of the finest châteaux in the Île de France and one of the major architectural influences on Versailles.

Chantilly *

48km (30 miles) north of Paris (SNCF from Gare du Nord to Chantilly-Gouvrieux)

Two Renaissance châteaux stand side by side in magnificent gardens, laid out in 1662 by Le Nôtre. The décor and furnishings are dazzling, but the prize exhibit is the priceless 15th-century illuminated manuscript, *Les Très Riches Heures du Duc de Berry*. Chantilly also has one of the premier racecourses in France.

Giverny *

76km (47 miles) northwest of Paris (SNCF from Gare St Lazare to Vernon, then a taxi)

Claude Monet, arguably the greatest of all the Impressionists, lived in this simple house, still crammed with his memorabilia, from 1883 until he died in 1926, creating the luxuriant garden which he then painted and repainted, above all in his most famous series, *Décorations des Nymphéas* (Waterlilies), his canvases becoming bigger and more abstract as he gradually lost his sight.

Thoiry

40km (25 miles) west of Paris (SNCF from Gare de Montparnasse to Montfort l'Amaury, then a bus or taxi)

There is something for everyone here, with a finely furnished château, built in 1564, and now also housing the **Musée des Archives**, 100ha (250 acres) of beautiful gardens with areas of both formal French patterning and English-style parkland, an extensive wildlife park with lions, tigers, elephants, rhinos, crocodiles, bears etc., along with gentler creatures and birds, a toy road train and park for miniature animals.

AUVERS-SUR-OISE

40km (25 miles) northwest of Paris (RER Line A to Cergy-Préfecture, then a shuttle bus)
This delightful village was beloved by many Impressionist painters including Pissarro, Corot, Daubigny and Renoir. Here you can visit Van Gogh's grave and the room where he died in 1890. A sophisticated multimedia tour, dedicated to the lives and works of these great artists, is housed in the 17th-century Château d'Auvers.

Below: *Monet used his water garden at Giverny as subject matter for many paintings, in particular his magnificent waterlily series.*

Paris at a Glance

Paris Info, 25 rue des Pyramides, 75001, Paris *(RER: Auber; metro Pyramides)*, tel: 08 92 68 30 00, web: www. parisinfo.com Open 10:00–19:00 Mon–Sat, 11:00–19:00 Sun. Everything you need under one roof. There are also offices at Opéra-Grands Magasins, Gare de Lyon, Eiffel Tower, Gare du Nord, Montmarte and Carrousel du Louvre.

Paris Île de France Information, Carrousel du Louvre, 99 rue de Rivoli, tel: 08 26 16 66 66, web: www. paris-ile-de-france.com

Paris has an excellent public transport network made up of the metro, buses (both run by RATP), RER and suburban mainline rail services (run by SNCF).

Tickets
Use same tickets on all transport. Paris is divided into 8 concentric zones; punch more tickets if you are travelling further. Single tickets are expensive, buy a *carnet* of 10 for a 30 per cent discount. Cheaper still are various passes – the 1 day **Mobilis** (all 8 zones); 1–5 day **Paris Visite** (various zones); and weekly (Mon–Sun) or monthly (from 1st of month) **Carte Orange** (ID and passport photos required). The cost goes up with the number of zones included (most major sights are within Zones 1–3; Versailles, Disneyland and

the airports are in Zone 5).

Tickets are available at main metro, RER and SNCF stations; Mobilis and *carnets* at some tabacs; Paris Visite and Mobilis at the main tourist office and airports.

Maison de la RATP, 54 quai de la Rapée, 75599, Paris, tel: 08 92 68 77 14, web: www. ratp.info *(metro: Gare de Lyon)*. Open 08:15–18:30 Mon–Thu, 08:15–18:00 Fri.

SNCF, tel: 08 36 35 35 35, web: www.sncf.com

Maps
Paris Plan des Lignes (Map 1) is an excellent, free transport map. Several department stores sponsor good, free street maps. *Paris par Arrondissement* is the best of several more detailed street atlases, sold in bookshops and news stalls.

The Metro
The metro has 370 stations. Trains run every couple of minutes from about 05:30–01:00. Lines are numbered and colour coded on maps, and named according to the last stop on the line. To change lines, trace the route to the last stop in the right direction and follow the *Correspondance* sign.

The RER
Five suburban rail lines, A, B, C, D and E. There are stops in the centre but most useful for longer journeys.

Buses
Good services during the day, stopping or tailing off after 20:30 and on Sunday. Bus routes and zones are displayed at bus stops and on the sides of the buses. You may have to use more than one ticket for a journey. Put single tickets through the punch machine as you board. *Do not* put your pass through the machine – just show it to the driver.

Restricted night bus service (Noctambus): 01:00–05:00; 18 lines fan out from place du Châtelet and av Victoria to the suburbs. One bus an hour each way on each route.

Taxis
Street hailing is allowed, but rarely successful at night. Licensed taxis show a white rooflight if available, an orange one if occupied. Three price bands – 07:00–19:00 Mon–Sat; 19:00–07:00 Mon–Sat and all day Sun; a higher charge for trips to the suburbs. Also supplements at stations, Air France

PARIS	J	F	M	A	M	J	J	A	S	O	N	D
AV. MAX TEMP. °C	6	7	12	16	20	23	25	24	21	16	10	7
AV. MIN TEMP. °C	1	1	4	6	10	13	15	14	12	8	5	2
AV. MAX TEMP. °F	43	45	54	60	68	73	76	75	70	60	50	44
AV. MIN TEMP. °F	34	34	39	43	49	55	58	58	53	46	40	36
RAINFALL mm	56	46	35	42	57	54	59	64	55	50	51	50
RAINFALL in	2.2	1.8	1.4	1.7	2.2	2.1	2.3	2.5	2.2	2	2	2
Days of Rainfall	17	14	12	13	12	12	12	13	13	13	15	16

Paris at a Glance

terminals, for luggage, more than three passengers and animals. Avoid unofficial taxis, which charge what they like. 24hr telephone bookings: **Alpha**, tel: 01 45 85 85 85; **G7**, tel: 01 47 39 47 39; **Taxis Bleus**, tel: 08 91 70 10 10, web: infotaxiparis.com

WHERE TO STAY

Paris accommodation is varied but not cheap. Most places charge per room rather than per person. Book ahead during peak seasons (spring, autumn). Check whether cheaper hotels take credit cards.

Accommodation Bureaux
Alcôve et Agapes, 8 bis rue Coysevox, 18th, tel: 01 44 85 06 05, fax: 01 44 85 06 14, web: www.bed-and-breakfast-in-paris.com e-mail: info@bed-and-breakfast-in-paris.com Singles and doubles bed and breakfast from 50–120 euros.
France Lodge Locations, 2 rue Meissonier, 17th, tel: 01 56 33 85 85, fax: 01 56 33 85 89, web: www.paris-rental.com *(metro: Wagram)*. Non-profit organization arranges accommodation in private homes and apartments from about 25 euros per person per night, plus a wide range of longer-stay holiday apartments.
     The main tourist office and the one at Gare de Lyon have a hotels reservation desk. Almost all major international chains have at least one hotel in the city. The French **Accor Group** (Formule, Novotel, Mercure,

Libertel, Ibis and Sofitel chains) has dozens of properties in Paris, tel: 01 60 77 27 27, web: www.accorhotels.com while **Timhotel** has 15; tel: 01 44 15 81 15, web: www.timhotel

Youth Accommodation
Fédération Unie des Auberges de Jeunesse (HI), 24 bd Jules Ferry 11th, tel: 01 43 57 02 60, fax: 01 40 21 79 92, web: www.fuaj.fr *(metro: République)*. Central Reservation office for all Hostelling International affiliates. Open daily 08:00–22:00.
HipHop Hostels, web: www. hiphophostels.com Excellent website with details of and connections to eight of the best youth hostels in Paris. Prices from 15 euros.
Hôtels des Jeunes (MIJE), Le Fauconnier, 11 rue du Fauconnier, tel: 01 42 74 23 45; Le Fourcy, 6 rue de Fourcy, tel: 01 42 74 23 45; Maubisson, 12 rue des Barres, tel: 01 42 74 23 45; Jean Monnet, 6 rue de Fourcy, tel: 01 43 13 17 00. Four hostels in the Marais *(metro: St-Paul, Pont Marie)*. All former aristocratic residences.

Palace Hotels
These few hotels are so famous and plushy they are tourist attractions in their own right. All very expensive.
Le Bristol Paris, 112 rue du Faubourg St-Honoré, 8th, tel: 01 53 43 43 00, web: www.lebristolparis.com *(metro: Miromesnil)*.

Le Crillon, 10 place de la Concorde, 8th, tel: 01 44 71 15 00, web: www.crillon.com *(metro: Concorde)*.
Four Seasons George V, 31 av George V, 8th, tel: 01 49 52 70 00, web: www.fourseasons.com *(metro: George V)*.
Le Grand Inter-Continental, 2 rue Scribe, 2nd, tel: 01 40 07 32 32, fax: 01 42 66 12 51, web: www.interconti.com *(metro: Opéra)*.
The Plaza Athénée, 25 av Montaigne, 8th, tel: 01 53 67 66 65, web: www.plaza-athenee-paris.com *(metro: Franklin D. Roosevelt)*.
The Ritz, 15 place Vendôme, 1st, tel: 01 43 16 30 30, web: www.ritzparis.com *(metro: Tuileries)*.

The Islands
A wonderful area – central yet peaceful; well situated for food, evening strolls and sightseeing.
Luxury
Jeu de Paume, 54 rue St-Louis en l'Île, 4th, tel: 01 43 26 14 18, web: www.jeudepaumehotel.com *(metro: Pont Marie)*. A 17th-century *jeu de paume* (early tennis) court now oozing discreet luxury.
Mid-range
Deux Îles, 59 rue St Louis en l'Île, 4th, tel: 01 43 26 13 35, *(metro: Pont Marie)*. Charmingly converted 17th-century mansion.
Budget
Henri IV, 25 place Dauphine, Île de la Cité, 1st, tel: 01 43 54 44 53, *(metro: Cité)*. Very simple and very popular.

Paris at a Glance

Beaubourg, Les Halles, the Marais and Bastille
An excellent area with numerous small hotels – central, pleasant for strolling and filled with charming eateries.
Luxury
Pavillon de la Reine, 28 place des Vosges, 3rd, tel: 01 40 29 19 19, web: www.pavillon-de-la-reine.com (*metro: Chemin Vert, St-Paul*). Small, elegant courtyard mansion rebuilt to original plans in one of the city's most beautiful squares.
La Bretonnerie, 22 rue Ste-Croix-de-la-Bretonnerie, 4th, tel: 01 48 87 77 63, web: www.brettonnerie.com (*metro: Hôtel de Ville*). Small, comfortable 17th-century hotel.
Mid-range
St-Merry, 78 rue de la Verrerie, 4th, tel: 01 42 78 14 15, web: www.hotelmarais. com (*metro: Hôtel de Ville*). 17th-century presbytery and 19th-century brothel, stylishly converted and furnished with Gothic bric-à-brac.
Budget
Castex, 5 rue Castex, 4th, tel: 01 42 72 31 52, web: www.castex-paris-hotel.com (*metro: Bastille*). Popular, cheap and cheerful.

Montmartre and the Northeast
A little way out, but perfect for those on a moderate budget; vibrant nightlife. Many cheap hotels, especially near the stations, some handling rough trade.

Luxury
Terrass Hôtel, 12 rue Joseph-de-Maistre, 18th, tel: 01 44 92 34 14, web: www.terass-hotel. com (*metro: Blanche*). Charmingly decorated, a good restaurant and excellent views.
Mid-range
Villa Royale, 2 rue Duperré, 9th, tel: 01 55 31 78 78, e-mail: royale@leshotelsde-paris.com (*metro: Pigalle*). Perhaps not the most salubrious area, but this hotel in a historic building is a charming riot of colour with friendly service.
Budget
Prima Lépic, 29 rue Lépic, 18th, tel: 01 46 06 44 64, fax: 01 46 06 66 11, (*metro: Blanche*). Bright and airy townhouse hotel in the heart of Montmartre.

The Louvre and Opéra
Convenient but uninspiring area. Excellent for shopping, lousy for nightlife, though the palace hotels near the Louvre create their own glamour.
Luxury
Régina, 2 place des Pyramides, 1st, tel: 01 42 60 31 10, web: www.regina-hotel.com (*metro: Pyramides*). Delightful Art Deco building filled with antiques.
Tuileries, 10 rue St-Hyacinthe, 1st, tel: 01 42 61 04 17, (*metro: Tuileries*).
Mid-range
Gaillon-Opéra, 9 rue Gaillon, 2nd, tel: 01 47 42 47 74, web: www.bestwestern.com (*metro: Opéra*). Warmly welcoming 19th-century building; wooden beams and flowery curtains.

Northwest Paris: The Rive Droite
Home to some of the finest hotels in Paris, dripping with money and celebrities. Nightlife centred on the Champs-Élysées. Not for those on tight budgets.
Luxury
Balzac, 6 rue Balzac, 8th, tel: 01 55 33 16 55, (*metro: George V*). Small, discreet, but extremely luxurious, with an excellent restaurant.
Hôtel Costes K, 81 av Kleber, 16th, tel: 01 44 05 75 75, fax: 01 44 05 74 74, e-mail: costes.k@wanadoo.fr (*metro: Trocadéro*). Ultra-chic, ultra-modern boutique hotel with cool art, hip staff and a central Japanese courtyard.
Mid-range
Résidence Lord Byron, 5 rue Châteaubriand, 8th, tel: 01 43 59 12 12, (*metro: George V*). Pleasant small courtyard hotel.

The Eiffel Tower, Les Invalides and the Musée d'Orsay
Fairly quiet and sober, this area is still splendidly central and prices are considerably lower than across the river.
Luxury
Duc de St-Simon, 14 rue de St-Simon, 7th, tel: 01 44 39 20 20, e-mail: duc.de.saint.simon @wanadoo.fr (*metro: Rue du Bac*). Elegant, welcoming hotel; small, flourishing garden.
Mid-range
Le Pavillon, 54 rue St-Dominique, 7th, tel: 01 45 51 42 87, (*metro: Latour Mau-*

Paris at a Glance

bourg). Former convent; tiny rooms andabundant charm.
Thoumieux, 79 rue St-Dominique, 7th, tel: 01 47 05 49 75, web: www.thoumieux. com *(metro: La Tour Maubourg)*. Ten comfortable, but simply furnished rooms, attached to a lively bistro.

The Rive Gauche and Montparnasse
Lively and entertaining area with numerous comfortable, middle-of-the-range hotels and wall-to-wall restaurants. An excellent place to stay.
Luxury
L'Hôtel, 13 rue des Beaux-Arts, 6th, tel: 01 44 41 99 00, web: www.l-hotel.com *(metro: St-Germain-des-Prés)*. Oscar Wilde died here in 1900. The hotel has come a long way since then. Contains beautiful furniture and a general air of extravagance. Renovated in 1968, each room has its own story. Room 16 is a reconstruction of Oscar Wilde's; room 36 has furniture belonging to music hall artist Mistinguett.
Hôtel d'Angleterre, 44 rue Jacob, 6th, tel: 01 42 60 34 72, *(metro: St-Germain-des-Prés)*. Once the British Embassy, later Hemingway's home. The treaty which ended the American War of Independence was prepared in this 18th-century building, although it was signed further up the street, as Franklin refused to set foot on British soil. Charming, comfortable, peaceful, surrounding a small flower-filled courtyard.

Mid-Range
Ste-Beuve, 9 rue Ste-Beuve, 6th, tel: 01 45 48 20 07, web: www.paris-hotel-charme.com *(metro: Vavin)*. This small hotel successfully mingles cool, understated elegance and a cosy, welcoming atmosphere.
Welcome Hotel, 66 rue de Seine, 6th, tel: 01 46 34 24 80, web: www.welcomehotel-paris.com *(metro: Odéon)*. Warm, friendly; on lively street; overlooks Buci flower market.
Esmeralda, 4 rue St-Julien-le-Pauvre, 5th, tel: 01 43 54 19 20, *(metro: St-Michel)*. Small 16th-century hotel with charmingly eccentric décor.

The Île de France
Disneyland Paris, Marne-la-Vallée/Chessy. Six huge theme hotels and a self-catering complex on site. Details and booking, tel: 01 60 30 60 30 or, in the UK, 0870 503 0303. Web: www.disneylandparis.com
Le Versailles, 7 rue Ste-Anne, Versailles, tel: 01 39 50 64 65, fax: 01 39 02 37 85, web: www.hotel-le-versailles.fr *(metro: Odéon)*. A friendly hotel near the château with spacious rooms, a pretty terrace and reasonable prices.

WHERE TO EAT

Paris has more restaurants per head than any other city in the world. The following list is only a minute fragment of all the wonderful options. As well as the individual restaurants, travellers on a moderate budget should take a look at some

of the chains of brasseries, such as **Hippopotamus** and the more upmarket **Flo** chain; **Léon le Bruxelles**; **Bistro Romain**; and **Bistrot d' à Côté** chain, which are cheaper eateries managed by some of the city's great chefs. *See* also pages 26–29.

The Islands
La Charlotte en Île, Rue St Louis en l'Île 24, 4th, tel: 01 43 54 25 83, *(metro: Pont Marie)*. Open 12:00–20:00, Thu–Sun. One of many lovely *salons de thé* (tearooms) on this street.
Le Vieux Bistro, 14 rue du Cloître Notre Dame, 4th, tel: 01 43 54 18 95, *(metro: Cité)*. The honourable exception to the normal lack of quality on the Île de la Cité. Traditional French cooking, warm friendly atmosphere. Moderate.
Brasserie de l'Île St Louis, 55 quai de Bourbon, 4th, tel: 01 43 54 02 59, *(metro: Pont Marie)*. Well-established, relaxed brasserie specializing in food from Alsace. Moderate.
Berthillon, 31 rue St Louis en l'Île, 4th, tel: 01 43 54 31 61, *(metro: Pont Marie)*. Said to produce the best ice cream in France. Approximately 60 different flavours, also sold in nearby cafés to cut the queues.

Beaubourg, Les Halles, the Marais and Bastille
L'Ambroisie, 9 place des Vosges, 4th, tel: 01 42 78 51 45, *(metro: St-Paul, Chemin Vert)*. A magnificent Michelin 3-star restaurant, in a superb

Paris at a Glance

setting. Book one month ahead. Very expensive.

Au Pied de Cochon, 6 rue Coquillière, 1st, tel: 01 40 13 77 00, (*metro: Les Halles*). A huge Paris institution, open 24hr. Set up originally to serve hearty fare to market workers, now the place to come for a breakfast of pig's trotters and onion soup after a heavy night out. Moderate.

Astier, 44 rue Jean-Pierre Timbaud, 11th, tel: 01 43 57 16 35, (*metro: Parmentier*). Great value prix-fixe menu with interesting traditional French food, a fabulous cheese board and wine list. Closed weekends. Reservations required. Moderate.

Bofinger, 5–7 rue de la Bastille, 4th, tel: 01 42 72 87 82, (*metro: Bastille*). Seafood specialist, with a 100-year pedigree and delightful Art Nouveau décor. Moderate.

L'Ambassade d'Auvergne, 22 ru du Grenier St-Lazarre, 3rd, tel: 01 42 72 31 22, (*metro: Rambuteau*). Lunch and dinners for the really hungry. Sausages and hams of this region are among the best in France.

Jo Goldenberg, 7 rue des Rosiers, 4th, tel: 01 48 87 20 46, (*metro: St-Paul*). The most famous Jewish deli and restaurant in Paris.

Le Trumilou, 84 quai de l'Hôtel de Ville, 4th, tel: 01 42 77 63 98, (*metro: Hôtel de Ville*). Authentic menu from the early 20th century. Open for lunch and dinner until

23:00 Mon–Sat and until 22:30 Sun.

Montmartre and the Northeast

La Famille, 41 rue des Trois-Frères, 18th, tel: 01 42 5211 12, (*metro: Abbesses*). Boho chic Basque restaurant with global influences. Dinner only; closed Sun–Mon. Moderate.

Brasserie Wepler, 14 place de Clichy, 18th, tel: 01 45 22 53 24, (*metro: Place Clichy*). Try the seafood at this 100-years-old brasserie. Moderate.

Chez Haynes, 3 rue Clauzel, 9th, tel: 01 48 78 40 63, (*metro: St-Georges*). One of the first American restaurants, with a jazz theme and soul food. Cheap.

Macis et Muscade, 110 rue Legendre, 17th, tel: 01 42 26 62 26, (*metro: La Fourche*). Excellent example of a *restaurant du quartier* (neighbourhood restaurant). Menu changes with the seasons; impeccable service. Open for lunch Sun, Tue–Fri, dinner until 22:30 or 23:00, Tue–Thu, Fri, Sat.

Le Soleil Gourmand, 10 rue Ravignan, 18th, tel: 01 42 51 00 50, (*metro: Abbesses*). Cheery little restaurant with warm décor; serves typical meridional dishes. Open for lunch and dinner until 23:00, Mon–Sat.

The Louvre and Opéra

Le Grand Véfour, 17 rue de Beaujolais, 1st, tel: 01 42 96 56 27, (*metro: Pyramides*).

Situated on the northern edge of the Jardin du Palais Royal and frequented by the Paris elite since 1784. Lunch and dinner menus (70–198 euros), open until 22:15, Mon–Fri.

Angelina's, 228 rue de Rivoli, 1st, tel: 01 42 60 82 00, (*metro: Tuileries*). Ultimate chic, a gilded tea room oozing with 19th-century charm. Expensive.

Chartier, 7 rue du Faubourg-Montmartre, 9th, tel: 01 47 70 86 29, (*metro: Rue-Mont-martre*). A cavernous barn set up in 1892 by the Communist Party to feed workers cheaply. Still offering good, cheap food, appalling service and spectacular Belle Epoque décor.

La Maison Savoureuse, 58 rue Sainte Anne, 2nd, tel: 01 42 60 03 22, (*metro: Quatre Septembre*). Cheap and cheerful; excellent value Vietnamese food. Wide choice for vegetarians. Sit or take-away.

Joe Allen, 40 rue Pierre Lescot, 1st, tel: 01 42 36 70 13, (*metro: Étienne Marcel*). Friendly American restaurant-bar; great atmosphere and excellent brunch (14.50–16.75 euros), 12:00–16:00, Sun. Also serves lunch and dinner.

Le Grand Colbert, 2–4 rue Vivienne, 2nd, tel: 01 42 86 87 88, (*metro: Bourse*). Charming, classic brasserie; opened in 1830; popular with theatrical crowd; open late; expensive.

Willi's Wine Bar, 13 rue des Petits-Champs, 1st, tel: 01 42 61 05 09, (*metro: Bourse*). English-run wine bar with pleasant décor, good wine and

Paris at a Glance

interesting menu. Moderate.
Aux Lyonnais, 32 rue St-Marc, 2nd, tel: 01 42 96 65 04, (*metro: Bourse*). Delightful bistro owned by mega-chef Alain Ducasse. Superb, constantly changing Lyonnais menu in charmingly old-fashioned surroundings. Closed Sun–Mon, Sat lunch. Moderate.

Also in this area are several palace hotels with superb dining rooms, among them the **Ritz**, **Inter-Continental**, and the **Bristol** (*see* Hotels, on page 114).

Northwest Paris: The Rive Droite
Fauchon, 30 place de la Madeleine, 8th, tel: 01 47 42 60 11, (*metro: Madeleine*). There are several eateries, from café to self-service to grand restaurant in this vast temple to food, headquarters of the Fauchon empire. Try the menu, then buy the ingredients. All price ranges.
L'Avenue, 41 av Montaigne, 8th, tel: 01 40 70 14 91, (*metro: Alma Marceau*). Art Deco restaurant with Provençale-inspired food, popular with fashion gurus. Moderate to expensive.
La Maison d'Alsace, 39 av des Champs-Élysées, 8th, tel: 01 53 93 97 00, (*metro: Franklin D. Roosevelt*). Huge, bright and busy brasserie, specializing in Alsatian food.
Lucas Carton, 9 place de la Madeleine, 8th, tel: 01 42 65 22 90, (*metro: Madeleine*).

Belle Epoque décor; innovative cuisine, 3 Michelin stars; book ahead; very expensive.
Maxim's, 3 rue Royale, 8th, tel: 01 42 65 27 94, (*metro: Concorde*). A Paris institution for nearly a century; the building is a national monument, the classic cuisine superb and the live music sophisticated. Book ahead. Very expensive.

This is the natural home of haute cuisine with a cluster of superb, vastly expensive restaurants, including **Chiberta**, **Laurent**, **Ledoyen**, **Taillevent**, and palace hotel dining rooms, amongst them the **Crillon**, **George V** and **Plaza Athénée** (*see* Hotels, on page 114).

The Eiffel Tower, Les Invalides, St-Germain and the Musée d'Orsay
Jules Verne, 2nd floor of the Eiffel Tower, 7th, tel: 01 45 55 61 44, (*metro: Bir-Hakeim*). The highest restaurant in Paris, and very popular with both tourists and Parisians. Book way ahead. The service is seamless and the traditional food excellent. Expensive.
Casa Corsa, 25 rue Mazarine, 6th, tel: 01 44 07 38 98, (*metro: Odéon*). Delicious Corsican cuisine. Simple and sophisticated. Open for lunch Tue–Sat, dinner until midnight Mon–Sat. Moderate.
À la Cour de Rohan, 59–61 rue St-André des Arts, 6th, tel: 01 43 25 79 67, (*metro: Mabillon*). A peaceful tea room with a delicious desert-cart

delicacies. Open 12:00–19:30 daily, 12:00–00:00 Fri and Sat, Apr–Oct.
Guen Maï, 2 bis rue de l'Abbaye, 6th, tel: 01 43 26 03 24, (*metro: St-Germain-des-Prés or Mabillon*). Cozy vegetarian restaurant serves organic daily specials (7.60–10 euros). Open 12:00–15:30 Mon–Sat.
Thoumieux, 79 rue St-Dominique, 7th, tel: 01 47 05 49 75, (*metro: Invalides*). A jolly bistro with hearty, country-style cuisine. Cheap.

The Rive Gauche and Montparnasse
A foodie's mecca, offering anything and everything from the sublime to the hamburger. For the best array of cheap and cheerful places in town, stroll the narrow pedestrianized streets behind **St-Julien le Pauvre** or in the area between **Place St-André-des-Arts** and **St-Germain-des-Prés**.
Brasserie Lipp, 151 boulevard St-Germain, 6th, tel: 01 45 48 53 91, (*metro: St-Germain-des-Prés*). Famous brasserie; clientèle has included the rich and famous from Hemingway to Madonna; 1920 décor is a national monument. Moderate.
Le Caméléon, 6 rue de Chevreuse, 6th, tel: 01 43 20 63 43, (*metro: Vavin*). A 'nouveau bistro' that serves fresh innovative food in a traditional setting. Open for lunch Mon–Fri, dinner until 23:00 Mon–Sat.
La Coupole, 102 boulevard du Montparnasse, 14th, tel: 01 43 20 14 20, (*metro: Vavin*). This

Paris at a Glance

huge brasserie was one of the great artists' hangouts of the 1920s and 30s and has been bustling ever since.

Le Kitch, 10 rue Oberkampf, 11th, tel: 01 40 21 94 14, (metro: Filles du Calvaire). Colourful Mediterranean-inspired food in a colourful and kitsch environment. Open for lunch Mon–Fri, dinner until 02:00 daily.

Le Bistrot du Dôme, 2 rue de la Bastille, 4th, tel: 01 48 04 88 44, (metro: Bastille). Charming, popular seafood restaurant. Blackboard menu changes daily. Open for lunch and dinner until 23:30 daily.

Le Procope, 13 rue de l'Ancienne Comédie, 6th, tel: 01 40 46 79 00, (metro: Odéon). Founded in 1686, this is one of the oldest and most famous cafés in Paris. During the Revolution it became the Café de Zoppi and the drinking haunt of the infamous Marat. Voltaire, Balzac and Verlaine were other habitués. Today visitors come to see the portrait of the infamous Dr Guillotin (yes, that one) and think historical thoughts as they eat. Traditional food, moderate prices.

La Tour d'Argent, 15-17 quai de la Tournelle, 5th, tel: 01 43 54 23 31, (metro: Maubert-Mutualité). One of the meccas of French gastronomy since 1582, the food is traditional French and about the best you will ever taste – the duck with cherries even comes with a numbered certificate. Book way ahead. Very expensive.

Perraudin, 157 rue St-Jacques, 5th, tel: 01 46 33 15 75, (RER: Luxembourg). A traditional bistro serving onion soup and boeuf bourguignon to local students. Cheap.

ENTERTAINMENT

Listings guides: l'Officiel des Spectacles and Pariscope (6-page English supplements) both available weekly on Wednesdays from any newsagent.

Kiosque Théâtre, has two outlets, one across from 15 place de la Madeleine, 8th, (metro: Madeleine), and the other on the parvis Mont-parnasse, 15th, (metro: Montparnasse Bienvenüe). They sell theatre tickets at half price (plus commission) on the day of any play, musical, concert, opera or ballet.

Virgin Megastore, 52–60 av des Champs-Élysées, 8th, tel: 01 49 53 50 00, (metro: Franklin D. Roosevelt). Wide-ranging booking agency handling everything from theatre to rock and sporting events.

You can also book by credit card on Minitel.

Cabaret
Moulin Rouge, 82 blvd de Clichy, place Blanche, 9th, tel: 01 53 09 82 82, (metro: Blanche).

Crazy Horse, 12 av George V, 8th, tel: 01 47 23 97 90, (metro: George V).

Lido de Paris, 116bis, av des Champs-Élysées, 8th, tel: 01 40 76 56 10, (metro: George V).

Theatre and Cinema
For French-speakers, there are numerous theatres, from the traditional to small experimental performance spaces. There are huge numbers of cinemas throughout the city, showing everything from Hollywood blockbusters to retrospectives and art films. VO (Version Originale) means it's sub-titled; VF (Version Française) means it's been dubbed.

Comédie Française, 2 rue de Richelieu, 1st, tel: 01 44 58 15 15, (metro: Palais-Royal). Great classic home of French drama.

Opera and Ballet
Opéra Bastille, 2–6 place de la Bastille, 12th, (metro: Bastille), tel: 08 92 89 90 90, web: www.operadeparis.fr for information and reservations.

Opéra-Garnier, place de l'Opéra, 2nd, tel: as above, (metro: Opéra). Cheap standby tickets on day of performance.

Music
There is always music available – on the streets, in the churches and museums, cafés, clubs and concert halls.

Classical concerts (sometimes free) held in several churches, including **Notre-Dame**, **Eglise du Val-de-Grâce**, **St-Julien-le-Pauvre** and **St-Eustache**, museums including the **Musée d'Art Moderne**, the **Musée de l'Homme** and in parks. Check handbills or see listings. **Cité de la Musique**, 221 av Jean-Jaurès, 19th, tel: 01 44 84 44 84, web:

Paris at a Glance

www.cite-musique.fr (*metro: Porte de Pantin*). Co-ordinates summer classical music festival.

TOURS

Bus

Paris Vision: 214 rue de Rivoli, 1st, tel: 01 42 60 30 01, (*metro: Tuileries*).

Cityrama: 4 place des Pyramides, 1st, tel: 01 44 55 61 00, (*metro: Pyramides*).

L'Open Tour: 13 rue Auber, 9th, tel: 01 42 66 56 56, website: www.paris-opentour.com (*metro: Havre Caumartin or Opéra*). Open-deck bus tours along three circuits: central Paris 2¼ hrs, Montmartre 1¼ hrs, Bastille–Bercy 1hr. Hop on and off at more than 40 stops. Schedules vary.

Boat

Bâteaux Mouches: Every 30min, 10:00–12:30 and 13:30–23:00, Mid-Mar–mid-Nov (rest of year 11:00, 14:30, 16:00 and 21:00 daily) from the Right Bank, Pont de l'Alma, (*metro: Alma Marceau*), tel: 01 42 25 96 10, website: www bateauxmouches.com Largest and best known of the sightseeing boats. Commentaries in French, German and English. Lunch (13:00) and dinner (20:30) cruises.

Bâteaux Parisiens: every 30min, 10:00–22:00 summer, hourly, 10:00–21:00 winter, from Port de la Bourdonnais, Pont d'Iéna, 7th, (*metro: Bir Hakeim/Trocadéro*), and Quai de Montebello, 5th, (*metro: Maubert-Mutualité/St-Michel*),

tel: 01 44 11 33 44. Lunch (12:15) and dinner (20:30) cruises .

Vedettes du Pont Neuf: every 30min, 10:30–23:00 summer, 09:00–22:00 winter, from the Square du Vert Galant, Île de la Cité, (*metro: Cité*), tel: 01 46 33 98 38. Discounts for Paris Visite ticket holders.

Batobus: unguided water bus every 25min. 8 stops at Eiffel Tower, Jardin des Plantes, the Louvre, Musée d'Orsay, Notre Dame, Hôtel de Ville, Champs-Élysées and St-Germain- des-Prés. April–Oct only, 10:00–19:00, tel: 01 44 11 33 99.

Canal trips

Paris Canal Croisiéres: 3hr cruise on the Seine and Canal St-Martin. One per day each way, two on weekends and public holidays. Quai Anatole France, Musée d'Orsay (*RER: Musée d'Orsay*) and Parc de La Villette, *19–21 quai de la Loire, 19th*, tel: 01 42 40 96 97, (*metro: Jaurès*).

Canauxrama: 3hr cruise on the Canal St-Martin. two departures each way daily. Port de l'Arsenal, *opp. 50 blvd de la Bastille, 12th*, (*metro: Quai de la Rapée*); the Bassin de la Villette, *13 quai de la Loire, 19th*, tel: 01 42 39 15 00, (*metro: Jaurès*).

Paris on Two Wheels

Several companies offer bicycle rental and guided tours. Try **Paris à Vélo C'est Sympa!**: 4th, tel: 01 48 87 60 01, 9 rue Jacques Coeur.

Paris on Foot

Paris Walking Tours, operated by Oriel and Peter Caine, tel: 01 48 09 21 40.

Pariscope and **L'Official des Spectacles** list a number of themed walks (in French).

SIGHTSEEING

Few sights are free, and tickets can be expensive. Occasional discounts of up to 50 per cent for ISIC (international student) cards or Paris Visite tickets. The commercially run **Paris City Passport** offers a wide range of sightseeing discounts that remain valid until the end of the year in which you buy it. The best option is to buy a **Carte Musées-Monuments**. This 1, 3 or 5 day pass gives entry to 50 different monuments and museums, including all the most famous. Recoup the cost in 3–4 visits and avoid horrendous queues at major sights. On sale at all participating museums and monuments, tourist offices and main metro stations.

SHOPPING

Haute Couture

Triangle d'Or, 1st and 8th, (*metro: Franklin D Roosevelt or Alma Marceau*): On av Montaigne are Prada, 10; Dolce a Gabbana, 22; Valentino, 17; Christian Dior, 30; Celine, 36; Nina Ricci, 39; Chanel, 40; Gucci, 60; Thierry Mugler, 49. Nearby, on av George V, 8th are Balenciaga, 10; and Jean-Paul Gaultier, 44.

Paris at a Glance

Rue du Faubourg St-Honoré, 8th, (*metro: Madeleine or Concorde):* Hermès, 24; Yves Saint Laurent Rive Gauche, 38; Chloe, 54; Comme des Garçons, 54; Guy Laroche, 28.

Place des Victoires, 1st and 2nd, (*metro: Bourse or Sentier):* Kenzo, 3; Thierry Mugler, 8. Nearby at rue Etienne Marcel, 1st: Barbara Bui, 23; Yohji Yamamoto, 47.

Marais
Rue des Rosiers, (*metro: St-Paul*), place des Vosges, rue de Rivoli, rue de Turenne and rue des Francs Bourgeois have a number of interesting shops.

St-Germain and Odéon:
Clothing boutiques on blvd St-Germain, (*metro: St-Sulpice or St-Germain-des-Prés*) include: Armani, 149 and 195; Sonia Rykiel, 175.
Clothing, footwear and leather goods along rue du Cherche Midi inlude:
Fausto Santini, 4; JB Martin, 13 and Il Bisonte, 17.
La Goutte d'Or, 18th has a collection of shops and stalls.

Prêt-à-porter
Many famous couture houses have cheaper ready-to-wear showrooms on the Left Bank. Those after even greater bargains should look for *dégriffé* signs. These denote designer products with the original label cut out, which are sold off at vast discounts due to overproduction or slight shop soiling. Good hunting grounds include

Rue St-Placid, Rue des Saints-Pères, Boulevard St-Michel, and Rue du Vieux Colombier. Rue Bonaparte is **the** shopping street of the Left Bank, but lock up your credit cards and window shop.

English Language Bookshops
Abbey Bookshop, 29 rue de la Parcheminerie, 5th, tel: 01 46 33 16 24, (*metro: Cluny-la Sorbonne*).
Brentano's, 37 av de l'Opéra, 2nd, tel: 01 42 61 52 50, (*metro: Opéra*).
Espace IGN, 107 rue La Boétie, 8th, tel: 01 43 98 85 00, (*metro: Franklin D Roosevelt*).
Shakespeare & Co, 37 rue de la Bûcherie, 5th, tel: 01 43 26 96 50, (*metro: St-Michel*).
WH Smith, 248 rue de Rivoli, 1st, tel: 01 44 77 88 99, (*metro: Concorde*).
Librarie Ulysse, 26 rue St-Louis en L'Île, 4th, tel: 01 43 25 17 35, (*metro: Pont Marie*).
Village Voice, 6 rue Princesse, 6th, tel: 01 46 33 36 47, (*metro: Mabillon*).

Fleas, Stamps and Car Boots
As well as its many delectable food markets (*see* page 90), Paris also has a thriving collection of specialist markets. Stamp collectors should head for the **Marché aux Timbres**, cour Marigny, 8th, (*metro: Champs-Élysées-Clemenceau*), open Thu, Sat and Sun 09:00–19:00. Those after prints and second-hand books should trawl the many stalls along the

quays, on both sides of the river, near the Île de la Cité (*metro: Châtelet, St-Michel*), open daily. Grand-daddy of all the local flea markets, selling anything antique or merely second hand, including clothes, is at **St-Ouen** (*metro: Porte de Clignancourt*), open Sat–Mon 10:00–18:00. There are others, smaller, less touristy and with perhaps a remote chance of a bargain, at the **Porte de Vanves**, av Georges-Lafenestre and av Marc-Sangier (*metro: Porte de Vanves*), open Sat and Sun 07:00–18:00; and the **Porte de Montreuil**, ave du Professeur André Lemière (*metro: Porte de Montreuil*), open Sat–Mon 08:00–18:00.

The Perfect Picnic
Poilâne, 8 rue du Cherche-Midi, 6th, is reckoned by many to be the best bakery in Paris. The speciality is a large country loaf that has become so popular that it is known everywhere as a *poilâne*. At **Beatrix**, 42 rue Dauphine, 6th, the speciality is baguettes cooked in a proper wood-burning oven.

For picnic supplies try **Flo Prestige**, 10 rue St-Antoine, 4th, (*metro: Bastille*). For cheese, go to **Barthélémy**, 51 rue de Grenelle, 7th and for absolutely everything, wallow in glorious food at **Fauchon**, 30 place de la Madeleine, 8th. Another superb fromagerie is **Fromagerie Alléosse**, 13 rue Poncelet, 17th, (*metro: Charles de Gaulle-Étoile*).

Travel Tips

French Tourist Offices Abroad

Australia: 25 Bligh St, Level 20, Sydney, tel: 02 9231 5244; fax: 02 9221 8682.
Canada: 1981 Avenue McGill College, Ste 490, Montreal, Quebec H3A 2W9, tel: (514) 288 2026; fax: (514) 845 4868, e-mail: canada@franceguide.com
Ireland: 10 Suffolk St, Dublin 2, tel: (01) 560 235 235; fax: (01) 679 0814; email: info.ie@franceguide.com
South Africa: PO Box 41022, Craighall, tel: (011) 880 8062, fax : (011) 770 16 66, e-mail : mdfsa@frenchdoor.co.za
UK: 178 Piccadilly, London W1J 9AL, tel: (09068) 244 123; fax: (020) 7493 6594.
USA: 444 Madison Ave, 16th flr, New York, NY10020, tel: (410) 286 8310; fax: (212) 838 7855, e-mail: info.us@franceguide.com

Getting There
By Air
Flights to Paris from almost every country in the world. Direct scheduled services from many UK regional airports.

Airports:
Roissy-Charles de Gaulle, 23km (14 miles) northeast of Paris on autoroute A1. 24hr flight and other information, tel: 01 48 62 22 80.
Airport transfers: RER line B3, every 4–15min.

Air France coaches every 15min to Place Charles de Gaulle-Etoile and Porte Maillot; tel: 08 92 35 08 20.

RATP Roissybus services every 15min to Opéra-Garnier; tel: 01 49 25 61 87. Journey time is approximately 1hr.

Orly, 20km (12½ miles) south of Paris on autoroute A6. 24hr flight information, tel: 01 49 75 15 15.
Airport transfers:
RER Line C2 and B4. Air France coaches depart every 12min to Les Invalides and Gare Montparnasse, tel: 08 92 68 77 14. The journey takes approximately 35min.

RATP Orlybus every 15min to Place Denfert-Rochereau. RATP information, tel: 08 92 68 77 14.

By Train
Six main SNCF stations handle train services from all over France and also from most other European countries. All are served by metro and RER.

For enquiries regarding the SNCF's mainline time-tables, tel: 08 92 35 35 35; for information and reserva-tions for suburban services, tel: 08 36 68 77 14, web: www.sncf.fr
Paris-Nord, *15 rue de Dunkerque, 10th.* Eurostar services through the Channel Tunnel and some UK boat trains.
Paris-Saint-Lazare, *rue St-Lazare, 8th.* UK boat trains.
Paris-Est, *10 place du 11 novembre 1918, 10th.*
Paris-Montparnasse, *17 blvd de Vaugirard, 15th.*
Paris-Austerlitz, *blvd de l'Hôpital, 13th.*
Paris-Gare de Lyon, *place Louis Armand, 12th.*
Eurotunnel, tel: (UK) 08705 35 35 35, (France) 03 21 00 61 00, web: www.eurotunnel.com
Eurostar, tel: (UK) 08705 186 186, (France) 0 892 35 35 39, web: www.eurostar.com

Documents

EU and other European, US, Canadian and New Zealand citizens will need to have a current passport. Other nationals may require a visa and should therefore check with their nearest French embassy before departure. Drivers from Europe, North America, Australia and New Zealand can use their national driver's licence; others should get an international licence. A green card is required for all foreign vehicles.

When to go

Any time of year. The climate is probably best and Paris looks prettiest in May/June and September/October. These are prime tourist times and also the festival seasons. Always make your hotel bookings in advance. Avoid travelling on the last weekends in July and August, the beginning and end of the French school holidays. In August Parisians go to the country, and many of the smaller shops and hotels close, but the town is pleasantly empty.

National Holidays

New Year's Day (1 January), Easter Sunday and Monday, May Day (1 May), VE Day (8 May), Ascension Day, Whit Monday (Pentecost), Bastille Day (14 July), Assumption (15 August), All Saint's Day (1 November), Armistice Day (11 November), Christmas Day (25 December).

Communications

Post

Stamps from La Poste offices, open Mon–Fri 08:00–19:00, Sat 08:00–12:00, and tabacs. Post boxes are small, wall-mounted and yellow. The main post office, *52 rue du Louvre, 1st*; tel: 01 40 28 20 00 (*metro: Sentier, Les Halles*) is open 24hr for telephones and collecting *poste restante* mail.

Telephone

Most public telephones use stored value phone cards available from tabacs, tourist shops, etc. A few older phone booths use coins. Most boxes handle international calls and have multilingual instructions. Also phone from post offices, and many cafés have pay phones (for local calls only). It is possible to use many national charge cards (eg Mercury, BT, AT&T etc) and Call Direct.

To phone Paris from abroad, dial the particular country's international access code (often 00) followed by the international country code for France (33), and then omit the 0, dialling the number 1 and the eight following digits. So to call Paris 01 22 44 66 88 from London, you would dial: 00 33 1 22 44 66 88.

Emergencies

EU-wide emergency number – tel: 112.
Police – tel: 17.
Fire – tel: 18.
SAMU (ambulance) – tel: 15.
Emergency doctor – tel: 01 43 37 77 77.

Emergency dentist – tel: 01 43 37 51 00 or 01 42 61 12 00.
Lost Property Office, *36 rue des Morillons, 15th*, tel: 40 30 52 00, (*metro: Convention*).

Health

EU citizens are entitled to subsidized (not free) treatment. Fill in Form E111 (from DSS offices) before travelling. You will have to pay, then claim for reimbursement. Full travel insurance is advisable. France is safe and clean, the water is drinkable and no vaccinations are needed. Pharmacists can often treat minor ailments.
Pharmacie des Champs, Galerie des Champs, *84 av des Champs-Elysées, 8th*; tel: 01 45 62 02 41. This 24hr pharmacy is open seven days a week.

English-speaking hospitals

Hertford British Hospital, 3 rue Barbés, 92300 Levallois-Perret, tel: 01 46 39 22 22, (*metro: Anatole-France*).
American Hospital, 63 boulevard Victor Hugo, 92202 Neuilly-sur-Seine, tel: 01 46 41 25 25 (*metro: Porte-Maillot*). Both private and expensive; most public hospitals will have some English-speaking staff.

Insurance

A good travel insurance policy should cover all medical costs, including repatriation; the loss, theft or damage of any belongings and money; cancellation and delay; and third party damages should you cause an accident. Available from any reputable travel agent.

Safety

Paris is no more or less dangerous than any other major city. There are no real 'no-go' areas, although women should think twice about walking around the Gare du Nord/Pigalle area on their own at night. Otherwise, be sensible. Be careful crossing the roads – the traffic can be lethal. Don't carry all your money and valuables around with you; most hotels can provide a secure lock-up. Men should make sure their wallet is securely anchored in an inside pocket and women should use a handbag with a cross-shoulder strap and zip. Late at night keep to well-lit streets and if in doubt take a taxi.

French Embassies Abroad

Australia: 6 Perth Ave, Yarralumla, Canberra ACT 2600, tel: (06) 62 16 01 00; fax: (06) 62 16 01 27.
Canada: 42 Promenade Sussex, Ottawa Ontario K1M 2C9; tel: (613) 789 1795; fax: (613) 562 3735.
Ireland: 36 Ailesbury Road, Ballsbridge, Dublin 4, tel: (01) 277 5000; fax: (01) 277 5001.
New Zealand: Rural Bank Building, 13th floor, 34–42 Manners Street, Wellington; tel: (04) 384 2555; fax: (04) 384 2577; website: www.ambafrance-nz.org
South Africa: (Feb–Mar) 78 Queen Victoria Street, Cape Town, 8001, tel: (021) 422 1338; fax: (021) 426 1996. (Apr–Jan) 250 Melk Street, New Muckleneuk, Pretoria, 0181, tel: (012) 425 1600; fax: (012) 425 1609. Website: www.ambafrance-rsa.org
UK: 58 Knightsbridge, London SW1X 7JT, tel: (020) 7073 1000, fax: (020) 7073 1042.
USA: 4101 Reservoir Road, NW, Washington DC 20007, tel: (202) 944 6000; fax: (202) 944 6166.

Embassies and Consulates in Paris

Australia, *4 rue Jean Rey, 15th*; tel: 01 40 59 33 00

(*metro: Bir Hakeim*).
Canada, *35 av Montaigne, 8th*; tel: 01 44 43 29 00 (*metro: Franklin D. Roosevelt*).
Ireland, *4 rue Rude, 16th*; tel: 01 44 17 67 00 (*metro: Argentine*).
New Zealand, *7ter rue Léonard-da-Vinci, 16th*; tel: 01 45 01 43 43 (*metro: Victor Hugo*).
South Africa, *59 quai d'Orsay, 9th*, tel: 01 53 59 23 23 (*metro: Invalides*).
UK, *35 rue Faubourg St-Honoré, 8th*; tel: 01 44 51 31 00 (*metro: Concorde*). Embassy: *35 rue du Faubourg St-Honoré, 8th*; tel: 01 44 51 31 00 (*metro: Concorde*). Consulate: *18 bis rue d'Anjou, 8th;* tel: 01 44 51 31 00, (*metro: Concorde*); open 09:30–12:30 and 14:30–17:00.
USA, Embassy: *2 ave Gabriel, 8th*; tel: 01 43 12 22 22, (*metro: Concorde*). Consulate: *2 rue St-Florentin, 1st;* tel: 08 10 26 46 26, (*metro: Concorde*).

Money

The currency is the euro, divided into 100 cents (called centimes here). Credit cards are widely accepted. Central banks are open Mon–Fri 09:00–16:30. Some branches are open on Sat, but close on Mon; many close 12:00–14:00 for lunch.
American Express: Main Office, *11, rue Scribe, 9th*; tel: 01 47 77 79 28 (*metro: Opéra; RER: Auber*). Open Mon–Sat 09:00–18:30. For lost or stolen travellers cheques, tel: 0 800 90 86 00.

CONVERSION CHART		
FROM	**TO**	**MULTIPLY BY**
Millimetres	inches	0.0394
Metres	yards	1.0936
Metres	feet	3.281
Kilometres	miles	0.6214
Hectares	acres	2.471
Litres	pints	1.760
Kilograms	pounds	2.205
Tonnes	tons	0.984

To convert Celsius to Fahrenheit: x 9 ÷ 5 + 32

FURTHER READING

Gilles Desmons, *Walking Paris*, New Holland Publishers, London, 1994: Detailed descriptions of 30 walks in and around the city. Anne and Alain Riou (annual), *Paris Pas Cher*, Editions du Seuil, Paris. Excellent listings guide to bargains from theatre tickets to couturier gowns. French. *Guide Gault Millau Paris* (annual). The city's top food and drink listings, crammed with other useful information. French. Robert Cole, *A Traveller's History of Paris*, Windrush, London, 1999: Easily digestible history of Paris from the year dot. John Ardagh, *France in the New Century: Portrait of a Changing Society*: A good introduction to modern-day France, its politics, its people and their idiosyncrasies. Ian Littlewood, *Paris: A Literary Companion*, John Murray, London, 1987: Anthology of great and not-so-great writings on the city. Raymond Rudorff, *Belle Epoque: Paris in the Nineties*, Hamish Hamilton, London, 1972: Gay Paris at the turn of the century. Victor Hugo, *Les Misérables*, Penguin Classics. Social injustice, revolution and a rousing story by the great 19th-century commentator on Paris. George Orwell, *Down and Out in London and Paris*, Penguin, London. Street life during the 1930s depression. Also novels by Honoré de Balzac, Emile Zola and Simone de Beauvoir, mostly available in English translation through Penguin Classics.

Thomas Cook: *Gare du Nord, 10th*; tel: 01 42 80 11 50 (*metro: Gare du Nord*). Open 06:15–23:30 daily. For lost or stolen travellers cheques, tel: 0 800 90 83 30 (24hr).

Tipping
Taxi drivers 10 per cent. Restaurant prices include all taxes and service charges, so leave small change only for exceptional service.

Electricity
220V, 2 round pin plugs. Sockets are always live, so don't leave things plugged in.

Time
GMT + 1hr in winter; + 2hr in summer.

Toilets
Standards and availability of public toilets have improved greatly over the last 10 years, and most are now squeaky clean. Available in selected metro stations, on the streets in the main tourist areas (often space-capsule style) and in all the cafés and bars, although you need to be quite brave to use these if you haven't bought anything. You may have to walk through the gents to reach the ladies. As ever, life is easier for men; women should keep a stash of coins handy.

Basic Vocabulary
Absolute Basics
Good morning/afternoon *Bonjour*
Good evening/night *Bon soir/bonne nuit*
Goodbye *Au revoir*
Sir (common usage for all men) *Monsieur*
Madam (common usage for all women) *Madame*
Yes *Oui*
No *Non*
OK *D'accord*
Please *S'il vous plaît*
Thank you (very much) *Merci (beaucoup)*
Excuse me/sorry *Pardon*
I don't understand *Je ne comprends pas*
Do you speak English? *Parlez-vous anglais?*
Do you have...? *Avez-vous/ Est-ce que vous avez...?*
How much is...? *Combien coûte...?*
When is...? *A quelle heure est...?*
Open *Ouvert*
Closed *Fermé*
Speak more slowly *Parlez plus lentement*
Write it down *Ecrivez-le*
Leave me alone *Laissez-moi tranquille*
Forbidden *Interdit*
Out of service *Hors de service/en panne*
Watch out! *Attention!*
Help! *Au secours/aidez-moi!*

Getting Around
Where is...? *Où est...?*
Left *Gauche*
Right *Droit*
Straight on *Tout droit*
Railway station *La gare*
Metro station *La station de métro*
Bus stop *L'arrêt du bus*

Platform *Le quai*
Ticket *Le billet*
One-way *Simple*
Return *Aller-retour*
Child's ticket *Un billet d'enfant*
Book of tickets *Un carnet*
Street plan *Un plan*
Map *Une carte*

Calendar

Monday *Lundi*
Tuesday *Mardi*
Wednesday *Mercredi*
Thursday *Jeudi*
Friday *Vendredi*
Saturday *Samedi*
Sunday *Dimanche*

January *Janvier*
February *Février*
March *Mars*
April *Avril*
May *Mai*
June *Juin*
July *Juillet*
August *Août*
September *Septembre*
October *Octobre*
November *Novembre*
December *Décembre*

Numbers

Half *Demi/la moitié*
One *Un*
Two *Deux*
Three *Trois*
Four *Quatre*
Five *Cinque*
Six *Six*
Seven *Sept*
Eight *Huit*
Nine *Neuf*
Ten *Dix*
Eleven *Onze*
Twelve *Douze*
Thirteen *Treize*
Fourteen *Quatorze*
Fifteen *Quinze*

Sixteen *Seize*
Seventeen *Dix-sept*
Eighteen *Dix-huit*
Nineteen *Dix-neuf*
Twenty *Vingt*
Thirty *Trente*
Hundred *Cent*
Thousand *Mille*

In the hotel

Floor (as in 2nd floor) *L'étage*
Lift (elevator) *L'ascenseur*
Room *La chambre*
Key *La clef/clé*
(Private) bathroom *La salle de bain (privée)*
Bath *Le bain*
Shower *La douche*
Toilet *La toilette; WC*
(Double) bed *Un (grand) lit*
Pillow *L'oreiller*
Air-conditioning *La climatisation*
Heating *Le chauffage*
...does not work *...ne marche pas.*

Mealtimes

Breakfast (included) *Le petit déjeuner (compris)*
Lunch *Le déjeuner*
Dinner *Le dîner*
Fixed-price meal *Le menu*
Dish of the day *Le plat du jour*
Starter *Hors d'oeuvres*
Soup *La soupe*
Main course *L'entrée*
Pudding *Le dessert*
Menu *La carte*
Bill *L'addition*
(Fizzy) Water *L'eau (gazeuse)*
Milk *Le lait*
Fruit juice *Le jus de fruit*
Tea *Le thé*
Herbal tea *La tisane*
Hot chocolate *Le chocolat chaud*
Coffee *Le café*

Black *Noir*
With cream *Le café crème*
With milk *Le Café au lait*
Wine *Le vin*
Red/white/rosé *Rouge/blanc/rosé*
Bread *Le pain*
Butter *Le beurre*
Meat *La viande*
Beef *Le boeuf*
Pork *Le porc*
Lamb *L'agneau*
Chicken *Le poulet*
Liver *Le foie*
Kidney *Le rognon*
Sweetbread *Le ris*
Blue (still mooing) *Bleu*
Rare *Saignant*
Medium *A point*
Well-done *Bien cuit*
Fish *Le poisson*
Hake *Le colin*
Trout *La truite*
Prawn *La crevette*
Oyster *La huître*
Snail *L'escargot*
Vegetarian *Végétarien*
Vegetables *Les légumes*
Potato *La pomme de terre*
Chips *Les frites*
Rice *Le riz*
(Green) beans *Les haricots (verts)*
Peas *Les petits pois*
Mixed salad *La salade mixte*
Tomato *La tomate*
Onion *L'oignon*
Lettuce *La laitue*
Cheese *Le fromage*
Ice-cream *La glace*
Apple *La pomme*
Orange *L'orange*
Lemon *Le citron*
Pear *Le poire*
Peach *La pêche*
Apricot *L'abricot*
Black currant *Le cassis*
Strawberry *La fraise*
Raspberry *La framboise*

INDEX

Page numbers in *italics* refer to captions accompanying illustrations